WHAT *if...*

DESTINY IMAGE BOOKS BY BENI JOHNSON

The Happy Intercessor

The Joy of Intercession

DESTINY IMAGE BOOKS BY THERESA DEDMON

Born to Create

WHAT *if...*

You Joined your
Dreams with the
Most Amazing GOD

BENI JOHNSON
SHERI SILK
THERESA DEDMON
DAWNA DESILVA
JENN JOHNSON
APRIL LAFRANCE
BRITTNEY SERPELL
JULIE WINTER

DESTINY IMAGE® PUBLISHERS, INC.
P.O. Box 310, Shippensburg, PA 17257-0310
"Promoting Inspired Lives."

This book and all other Destiny Image, Revival Press, MercyPlace, Fresh Bread, Destiny Image Fiction, and Treasure House books are available at Christian bookstores and distributors worldwide.

For a U.S. bookstore nearest you, call 1-800-722-6774.
For more information on foreign distributors, call 717-532-3040.
Reach us on the Internet: www.destinyimage.com.

ISBN 13 TP: 978-0-7684-0311-4
ISBN 13 Ebook: 978-0-7684-8775-6

For Worldwide Distribution, Printed in the U.S.A.
2 3 4 5 6 7 8 / 17 16 15 14 13

Endorsements

Few people get at the heart of a matter like Sheri does. Her keen understanding of people and her environment allow her to align with Heaven in a unique way that brings such strength and encouragement to all who hear her message. This contribution to *What If* is for those who need courage and hope to reach for and expect what they know God has put in their heart.

Danny Silk (Husband)
Senior Leadership Team, Bethel Church, Redding, CA
Author of *Culture of Honor* and *Loving Our Kids on Purpose*

CONTENTS

Introduction—What If You Could Live Your Destiny?
    Beni Johnson and Sheri Silk....................................9

Chapter 1—To Be Known
    Sheri Silk...13

Chapter 2—Children of Obedience
    Dawna DeSilva...25

Chapter 3—Smooth but Deadly
    Beni Johnson...39

Chapter 4—All of Heaven Is Celebrating You
    Theresa Dedmon 51

Chapter 5—Keeping It Real
    Jenn Johnson...65

Chapter 6—The Priority of Connection
    Sheri Silk and Brittney Serpell.....................77

Chapter 7—Finding Adam
    April LaFrance 91

Chapter 8—Renewed Thinking: Overcoming
       Mood Disorders
       Julie Winter..103

Chapter 9—Raising Discerning Kids
       Jenn Johnson..117

Chapter 10—Walking in God's Favor
       Dawna DeSilva...131

Destiny Prayers 143

What If You Could Live Your Destiny?

Beni Johnson and Sheri Silk

GOD HAS AN AMAZING, FULFILLING, life-changing purpose for each one of us. Unfortunately, too many women in the Church do not really know who they are or where they fit in God's Kingdom. They have accepted other people's molds and the status quo, but deep inside, they long for more. Their hearts secretly ask, *What if…? What if I could follow my dreams? What if I could do more than I'm doing and be more than I am right now? What if I could be really alive with purpose and participate in God's Kingdom? What if I could make a difference?*

The answer to these questions is "You can!" Because of Jesus, you are free to be amazing! You are free to follow your dreams! As a woman, you were created to be powerful and to step into your destiny as a world-changer. At Bethel Church in Redding, California, we are passionate about helping all kinds of people discover who

God created them to be and what He created them to do—and then empowering them to step into destiny.

We, the authors of this book, are women who carry various gifts and assignments and leadership roles; we know firsthand what it is like to encounter God's love and the joy and freedom of His presence. And from that place of encounter, we have begun to step into destiny. The same love and joy and freedom in God are available to you, too! He wants to change you in His presence—to free you of all the restraints that others and your own fears and sins have created—so that you can find who you really are in Him. Your identity and destiny in Him are much more exciting than you have ever imagined.

Understanding God's goodness and the freedom that's found in His love is the key to unlocking your destiny. The more you walk in your identity as a free woman, the more you will be able to discern and follow God's plans for your life. Free people dream with God. And only free people know they are powerful enough to turn those dreams into reality and become conduits of the Kingdom everywhere they go.

We are not all called to the same positions of influence or the same people groups, but we are all called, and we are all powerful beyond imagination. We can all do the work of the Kingdom—not one of us is disqualified because of race or gender or age or past failures. Freedom is what we were made for! We are designed to live out our destiny in partnership with God—to live every day and every year with bigger dreams. We really can change the world!

This book is written to help you discover your identity in God and to realize the powerful expectation residing in the question *What if?* The Bible declares that God *"is able to do exceedingly abundantly above all that we ask or think, according to the power that works in us"* (Eph. 3:20 NKJV). It also says, *"Eye has not seen, nor ear heard, nor have entered into the heart of man the things which*

God has prepared for those who love Him" (1 Cor. 2:9 NKJV). The limitation is not on His end, but on ours. Your Father is saying, "Permission granted!"

Imagine what might happen if you allowed God's love to truly penetrate your heart and you stopped being afraid of Him, afraid of others, and afraid of yourself. What if you actually received the spiritual, emotional, and physical wholeness that Jesus purchased for you on the cross? What might you do if you stopped being afraid of failure and started believing that God wants you to boldly pursue your dreams? The possibilities are limitless—and breathtaking!

Together, we are creating a Kingdom culture at Bethel, and through our stories and lessons, we invite you to do the same. We invite you to consider: *What if I could take hold of my destiny and join my dreams with the most amazing God? What if...?*

Chapter 1

To Be Known

Sheri Silk

ONE TIME OUR DAUGHTER, BRITTNEY, drove through the drive-through at the bank with her brothers in the car. They were laughing and having a good time together. When she pulled up to the window, Brittney placed her deposit slip and check into the little tube and sent it off. After the teller got it, she said over the loudspeaker, "Hi, Brittney, how are you today?"

"Good, thanks," Brittney said. Then she turned to her brothers and said, "They know me here. I come here all the time."

Her brothers snorted, "Yeah, right. They know your name because it's on your *check*, Brittney."

We all want to be *known*. Like Brittney, we like it when people call us by name, but we also want to know that they accept us—and even celebrate us. We need to be both recognized and received. It's great when people recognize us and know our names, but we long for more; we are hungry for evidence that they love us. We are long-ing for intimacy in our everyday lives.

The same is true in our relationship with God. At the core of who we are, we are longing to be known—and to know that we are known—by the One who created us. We have an innate need to be connected with God. David expressed this so well when he wrote, *"Search me, O God, and know my heart; Try me and know my anx-ious thoughts; And see if there be any hurtful way in me, And lead me in the everlasting way"* (Ps. 139:23-24 NASB).

SEARCH AND KNOW

When I gave my life to Jesus, I was only twenty-one years old, but prior to that, in my teen years, I had done a lot of damage to myself and to others. I got saved at the church that Bill Johnson pas-tored in Weaverville, and when I went forward to accept Jesus, I first asked Bill, "Will God want me if He really knows me?" I believed—as we so often do—that because I had done hurtful things, I was undesirable on the inside. I wanted to be known, but I was afraid that being known would result in being rejected. Other people had rejected me, and I thought God might, too—especially once He saw how yucky I was on the inside. It is easy to read Psalm 139:23 and feel afraid of the searching and knowing, but we don't need to. He's not searching in order to condemn us, but to cleanse us.

The *American Heritage Dictionary,* third edition, defines the word *search* as "to hunt, to look for, to investigate, explore, rum-mage around." I love the thought of God "rummaging around" in my heart—helping me find the parts of myself that I've lost or over-looked! As a woman who has been to the doctor many times and given birth to three children, I *know* in a very personal sense what *search* means! Any mother will testify that once she's had a baby, she has nothing left to hide. The most intimate parts of her body have been bared to examination, and that privacy that she had before motherhood no longer exists. This is how we are with God—our souls are bare before Him, and He examines us.

One of my favorite scenes from the movie, *The Last of the Mohicans,* powerfully explains this concept. At one point, several of the characters are hiding in a cave behind a waterfall; however, the enemy is coming. The hero, Nathaniel Hawkeye, knows he must leave because his presence will cause the death of them all. However, he does not want to leave them behind, especially not the lovely Cora. So before he jumps down the waterfall, he urges her, "You be strong, you survive...Stay alive, no matter what occurs. I will find you."[1] That sort of intensity, that sort of searching, is something our hearts long for. This is what God means when He says He will search us, and we don't need to be afraid of it.

I like to say that *intimacy* means "into me you see." Really, it means, "into me you see *because I showed you.*" It is an invitation to understand and to be familiar.

Of course, we can argue that God already knows everything about us. He created us, and He is all-knowing. That is true, but it is also true that He designed His relationship with us in such a way that we need to talk to Him and share ourselves with Him. He doesn't want a robotic knowledge of us. Rather, the desire in God's heart is to listen to us as we talk to Him—as we willingly open ourselves to Him. He wants us to share our hearts with Him, to invite Him in to "search" and "know." The truth is, we don't need to protect ourselves from God. After all, He is our provider and protector, our friend and lover, our counselor and comforter—and it's actually to our advantage to welcome Him in. Our prayer should be, "In to me You see, Lord, because I showed You. I don't need to protect myself from You. Instead, come search me and know me, be in charge of me and guide me, be ahead of me and influence me. I trust You."

NO NEED TO HIDE

As with all things, we have a choice. We can invite Him in, or we can say, "No way are You getting in here—to my heart—unless You forcefully enter." We don't need to be afraid of God's searching. What will He find that He doesn't already know? Nothing. But God doesn't want head knowledge about us; He already has that. And what He knows hasn't scared Him off. Rather, He wants to experience us; He wants to be welcomed into our hearts, which is the only way to have true intimacy with Him, no matter how much He knows about us.

So often we try to protect ourselves from others, including God. Marriage is a perfect example. A wife may long for her husband to truly know her, but instead of inviting him in and telling him what she needs, she makes him guess. And when he gets it wrong, she takes it as proof that she needs to protect herself from him because he doesn't really know her. I used to do this with my husband, Danny, a lot. I would use anger to protect myself from him because it made me feel powerful. I didn't realize that anger is false power and that true strength means being honest about what's going on and what I need.

For example, I used to get really angry at Danny when he would drive fast. I would yell at him, tell him the right way to drive, and tell him to consider the kids' safety (though, of course, they loved the fast driving). This just created a power struggle between me and Danny, and neither one of us was having fun. Eventually, though, I learned to look inside and ask myself why I was upset and what I needed. I realized that I didn't like Danny's fast driving because I didn't feel safe. And I found out that he responded a lot better when I told him, "You're scaring me, and I need you to slow down so I don't feel afraid," rather than simply yelling, "Slow down you idiot! You're driving too fast!"

Do you know how to tell God want you're feeling and what you need? Do you know how to talk to Him like He's a person—like He's your best friend? He wants you to stop protecting yourself from Him and to welcome Him in instead. He's listening for your invitation to intimacy; He wants to be that close to you.

KNOWING HIS VOICE

In John 10:11-14, Jesus gave us a picture of what He wants our relationship to look like:

> *I am the good shepherd; the good shepherd lays down His life for the sheep. He who is a hired hand, and not a shepherd, who is not the owner of the sheep, sees the wolf coming, and leaves the sheep and flees, and the wolf snatches them and scatters them. He flees because he is a hired hand and is not concerned about the sheep. I am the good shepherd, and I know My own and My own know Me* (NASB).

He wants to know us, and He wants us to know Him. He wants us to recognize His voice when He calls—like a good friend who needs no introduction on the phone. We all have friends like that, whose voices we instantly recognize. Jesus wants to be one of those friends.

The parable of the Good Shepherd reminds me of the time when Mary Magdalene first encountered Jesus after His death and resurrection. She didn't know He was alive, and she was standing by His tomb weeping for Him. When she turned around, she saw Jesus, but didn't recognize Him, thinking He was the gardener. He asked her who she was looking for, but she still didn't recognize Him—not until He said her name. *"Jesus said to her, 'Mary!' She turned and said to Him in Hebrew, 'Rabboni!' (which means, Teacher)"* (John 20:16 NASB). For whatever reason, Mary didn't recognize Him until He said her name—until He declared, "I know you! I see you! I love you!"

Mary had invited Jesus into her life and had loved Him extravagantly—so much so that Jesus chose her to be the first one to see Him after His resurrection. He chose her even above Peter and John (the disciple Jesus loved), waiting until they had fled before He revealed Himself. This is the sort of intimacy He longs for with each of us.

And though it may feel scary, we don't need to be afraid; He will not fail us like people do. When we get close to people, we discover their limits. No matter how amazing they are, they can't always be there when we need them. One of my top love languages is quality time. When I get home from work, I need to fill Danny in on everything that has happened since I last saw him. He does a great job caring, but he has his limit, and sometimes I talk and talk until his eyes glaze over from too much information. He's just human. Fortunately, God doesn't have a quality time limit with me or with you. Instead, He is able to be all things to all people—to love us in the way that blesses us the most.

LED BY LOVE

Connected to the idea of *searching* is the idea of *leading*. David ended his invitation to God to "search me" with the prayer, "… *and **lead me** in the everlasting way*" (Ps. 139:24 NASB). The result of being searched and known by God is being led by His love. God doesn't want to drag us along; in fact, He refuses to do that. He wants us to follow Him, to allow ourselves to be led by Him because we love Him.

Jeremiah 31 prophesies God's desire for people who will not run from Him, but who will follow Him because of love.

"Behold, days are coming," declares the Lord, "when I will make a new covenant with the house of Israel and with the house of Judah, not like the covenant which I made with their fathers in the day I took them by the hand to bring them out of the land of Egypt, My covenant which they broke, although I was a husband to them," declares the Lord. "But this is the covenant which I will make with the house of Israel after those days," declares the Lord, "I will put My law within them and on their heart I will write it; and I will be their God, and they shall be My people. They will not teach again, each man his neighbor and each man his brother, saying, 'Know the Lord,' for they will all know Me, from the least of them to the greatest of them," declares the Lord, "for I will forgive their iniquity, and their sin I will remember no more" (Jeremiah 31:31-34 NASB).

God is looking for people who will have a love relationship with Him, not just a contract. Not only does He want to know us, but He wants us to know Him. He says, *"…They will all know Me…."* That is the end goal of His searching and knowing—that in that place of intimacy we would fall in love with Him and begin to follow Him because of love.

WHO DO YOU SAY I AM?

In Matthew 16, Jesus showed us His desire to be known when He asked His disciples, "Who do you say that I am?"

When Jesus came into the district of Caesarea Philippi, He was asking His disciples, "Who do people say that the Son of Man is?"

So they said, some say John the Baptist; and others, Elijah; but still others, Jeremiah, or one of the prophets."

*He said to them, **"But who do you say that I am?"***

Simon Peter answered, "You are the Christ, the Son of the Living God."

And Jesus said to him, "Blessed are you, Simon Barjonah, because flesh and blood did not reveal this to you, but My Father who is in heaven (Matthew 16:13-17 NASB).

The people who didn't really know Jesus had their opinions. They had observed His actions and heard His words from a distance, and they had labeled Him incorrectly. They thought they knew Him, but they were wrong. Peter knew the right answer. He knew Jesus. And Jesus blessed him for being one who knew Him. You can hear the excitement in Jesus' blessing—the joy of being known. It is as though He is shouting, "Finally, you see Me! Finally, you are beginning to know and love Me!"

Don Potter wrote a song about this called "Who Do You Say I Am?" Years ago I heard him sing it at a MorningStar conference in Florida. As he was singing the verse, the spiritual energy was building in the room:

> Children come gather around, I have something I want to ask.
>
> We have loved those that didn't love first. We have tried to quench their thirst.

The first line is Jesus speaking, and the second is the disciples' answer. The verse goes on like this with several more questions and answers. All the while, the energy was building and building until Don Potter reached the chorus. He sang:

> Who do they say I am?
>
> Who do you say I am?

Who do they say I am?

Who do you say I am?

Suddenly, the lights went out. The electricity in the entire building shut down right as we were about to sing out the answer to "Who do you say I am?" The presence of God in that moment was incredible, and it was like God was asking us that same question—inviting us to really know Him. No one could see anything, and we were terrified and on our faces, wondering what was going to happen next.

Just as suddenly, the electricity returned, and the band, who had continued to play, even without their amps and microphones, picked up the song right where they'd left off.

Some say Elijah, some say John, but who do you say I am?

You are the Christ.

You are the Lord.

You are Messiah, God of all.

You are the master of all men.

Now I know "I AM."

You are the Lord.[2]

God is asking, "Who do you say I am?" Who is He in your life? Who do you tell people He is? We all long to be known for who we are. God is no different; He longs to be known by you.

REAL RELATIONSHIP

One day I talked with a man in his mid-thirties, a very successful businessman who earns a triple-digit income. He has a nice family, and he provides for them very well. He told me about his dad, saying, "My dad always wants to know about my job. He wants to know about how much money I make, what I own, what I drive—but he never wants to know who I am."

This man does drive a nice car, but that's not what he wants to be known and valued for. He'd rather his dad asked him about his heart, his thoughts, his dreams—the things that really define who he is. We can all relate to this desire to be known, not for our achievements or possessions, but because of who we are on the inside. We want love that sticks around, even when what we do or have is not that exciting.

Fortunately, unlike this man's father, you have a Father who cares about the real you and wants to search and know you intimately. He is awaiting your invitation. Have you talked with Him recently—I mean *really* talked with Him? Or do your friends know you better than He does? You don't necessarily have to use words. God doesn't need words to speak to you; He communicates His love in many ways.

Danny and I have a strong marriage. We've invested a lot of time and energy into making *us* work, and when we're sitting in a meeting and lots of other important stuff is happening around us, I can look into his eyes and feel his love for me without any words being spoken. We don't need words. When my mom was dying of cancer, toward the end, she couldn't talk very well. So I would just lay on her bed with her and look into her eyes. She would reach across the pillow and rub her thumb against my cheek. We didn't need words. A glance or a touch can say it all—can say, "I see you. I know you're here, and you matter to me. I know who you are and what you care about."

We all have friends with whom we have this sort of connection. The question is, do we have this sort of connection with God? God knows everything about us already, but if we want that deep connection with Him, we need to tell Him the intimate things in our hearts. Knowing about a person is not the same as intimately knowing a person. We can't keep secrets from God because He's God, but a relationship with Him is always a choice. Knowing is about relationship, and that's why He wants an invitation. That's why He wants to hear the details of our thoughts and dreams *from us.*

GREATER ACCESS

One of the perks of intimacy is greater access. When I know someone well, I am allowed deeper. I am given special privileges in our relationship that not just anyone can have. Some people I keep at a distance, some I allow a little closer, and others can come right in. The more I share my heart with a person, the more access that person has to me because I trust that person really knows me and will protect the things that matter to me.

When our kids were still living at home, they enjoyed full access to Bethel events. When Bethel would have a conference, our son Taylor would flip over his name badge (which was his ticket into the event) and write, "Danny Silk's son, all access." That meant he was no longer restricted to the main conference rooms, but he could go eat the food in the Hospitality Room if he wanted. He had full access because he was a son, and he wasn't afraid to take advantage of it.

Children have an amazing revelation of this truth. They don't question, "Is this an okay time to climb into Daddy's lap?" No, they just go for it. They know they have full access—anytime. God wants us to know Him and be known by Him to that extent. He wants us to feel so comfortable in our intimacy with Him that we can just "climb up in His lap" anytime. As His children, we have full access to Him, and the deeper we go with Him, the more we find that His lap is the safest and best place for solving life's problems and finding healing.

It is the very best place in the whole world, but if you feel afraid of intimacy—of being searched and known—you won't go there. You'll try to hide and protect yourself, and you'll miss out on access to the best relationship you could ever have. Don't miss it. Invite God to search you, to know you, and to lead you. No matter what's going on inside of you, God is not afraid of it. Whether you're ashamed because of sin in your life or you're bursting with dreams and ideas, He wants to hear it. He wants you to tell Him about yourself—to invite Him inside your guts. So stop being afraid of Him and realize who you are. He wants you to come to Him as a child, with full access, because He wants to know you and to be known by you. He wants to give you His heart.

Endnotes

1. *The Last of the Mohicans,* Michael Mann, dir. (Ashville, NC: Morgan Creek Productions, 1992), based on the novel by James Fennimore Cooper.

2. Don Potter, "Who Do You Say I Am?"; http://www.lyricstime.com/don-potter-who-do-you-say-i-am-lyrics.html (accessed April 27, 2012).

Chapter 2

CHILDREN OF OBEDIENCE

Dawna DeSilva

WHEN MY BOYS WERE YOUNG, I worked from home in the afternoons, tutoring high school students in German, French, and Spanish. One day, I spent the entire morning picking up toys and cleaning our house. Everything was in its place: The dishes were in the cupboard, the clothes were all folded and neatly tucked away, and all of the toys were separated into little, stacked plastic bins in the boys' closet.

Before my student came that afternoon, I told the boys to play quietly in their room and to not make a mess while mommy was working. However, about ten minutes into my tutoring session, I heard a loud crash followed by small, continuous rumblings coming from the boys' room. I got up to check on the situation and found Tim sitting on the floor near his closet surrounded by *all* of the toys that I had previously gathered into the neat plastic bins.

"Timothy James DeSilva..." I began. Then, just as I was crossing his bedroom floor, the rational thought came to mind that maybe this wasn't something my strong-willed two-year-old had done on purpose to challenge me. Perhaps he had been quietly trying to reach a toy from the top bin and had simply toppled it all over when he leaned in to take hold of his prize.

So, mid-stride, I stopped myself and loudly asked, "Timothy, was this an accident or was it on purpose?" Now I know that's a silly thing to ask a child, but I was trying to determine if this was another of his rebellious acts or perhaps truly a non-planned consequence.

He looked up at me, then back down at his toys, seeming to ignore me. Now I was really revving up! I was ready to "punish all disobedience," when he looked up at me again with the most innocent face and asked, "Mommy, which one doesn't get the swat?"

Isn't that how it is with us and God? So many of us obey Him because we fear getting a "swat," not because we understand that God has our best in mind—that He's working for our protection and our destiny. Do we follow His lead because we are afraid to misstep—to fail? Or do we follow Him because we know His steps lead us to still waters where He restores our souls? Unfortunately, many of us follow Him out of fear, and we miss the revelation that obedience, rather than being a measuring stick of our performance, is actually intended as a weapon in our hands for the "tearing down of strongholds."

Just the word *obedience* can make many people nervous or fearful because obedience has been so perverted by people to mean obeying at all costs—even to the point of receiving harm from those we are obeying. Some have come from abusive homes where they were not given a voice to say "no" to the bullies who were living side-by-side with them, causing them daily harm. Others have submitted with unholy or unhealthy submission, to the point that they have completely closed off their hearts from trusting an authority again.

If that is you, I challenge you to hear what I am saying in this chapter. Do *not* let the enemy win one more day! Instead, chose to open your eyes to see that perversion of authority has been the enemy's tactic to steal from you an extremely valuable weapon that can help you win the battle in your mind. You see, I believe the key to turning off the enemy's voice, the lies that he speaks into our minds, rests in our ability to correctly submit to safe authority and to walk as children of obedience.

Here is my prayer for you:

Lord, I pray that those who are reading this chapter—who are beginning to tune me out and are being tempted to put the book down—would take a moment to inquire of You and to hear Your prompting. Lord, give these readers the courage to forgive their abusers (and even themselves, if necessary) and to release any judgments they have made against themselves, others, or even You, God. As they bravely release their pain, I ask that You would open their spirits to receive the truth of this mighty weapon that they are about to wield!

WIELDING THE WEAPON OF OBEDIENCE

We all face moments of discouragement when we are bombarded by lies from the enemy. Even the great heroes of the Bible had to make a choice about what voice to listen to. Imagine what would have happened if Moses had continued to listen to the voice of discouragement when God called him to lead the Israelites out of Egypt. Imagine what may have happened if Paul had listened to the voice of the religious spirit when he faced persecution. They would have missed walking out the destiny that God had placed before them. They were called to be world-changers, and fortunately, they followed that call. They chose to obey God's voice and to silence the lies of the enemy, and we can too.

The question you have to consider is: What if you keep listening to the enemy's voice every time God asks *you* to do something? Or what if your obedience actually could shut those voices up?

Once we walk away from wrong, abusive obedience, we can walk into right obedience. And then we can turn proper obedience into the weapon that God intended it to be and actually begin defeating the enemy. To do that, first we need to understand the significance of obedience, and second, we need to have the courage to walk it out under safe, loving authority.

Before you read the verses below, take a moment to take off the lenses of distrust, pain, abuse, and bitterness. After you have given these perceptions to God, look at the following Scriptures:

> *Then Moses and the Levitical priests spoke to all Israel, saying, "Be silent and listen, O Israel! This day you have become a people for the Lord your God. You shall therefore obey the Lord your God, and do His commandments and His statutes which I command you today"* (Deuteronomy 27:9-10 NASB).

> *Obey your leaders and submit to them, for they keep watch over your souls as those who will give an account. Let them do this with joy and not with grief, for this would be unprofitable for you* (Hebrews 13:17 NASB).

> *Samuel said, "Has the LORD as much delight in burnt offerings and sacrifices as in obeying the voice of the LORD? Behold, to obey is better than sacrifice, and to heed than the fat of rams"* (1 Samuel 15:22 NASB).

These verses show us a lot about God's perspective on obedience. However, the tone we hear when we read them is completely dependent upon our lens for authority—whether we view it as benevolent or dictatorial. To help us break out of our negative lenses, let's consider obedience to God in the light of one of the Bible's most common metaphors—God the Father. As a good father, God does not delight in telling His children, "I told you so!" when they are distressed or in tears about a choice they made—even though His Word has clearly stressed, "Do not do that!" No, rather it breaks His heart to see His children facing the consequences of not heeding His advice.

God is not a heavy-handed, unsafe authoritarian who wants to use His position to cause us harm. He is not like the abusive father, brother, or family "friend" so many of us have been wounded by. Neither is He a dictatorial boss who allows us no voice or choice. He is the true lover of our souls, and He wants us to trust that His heart is for us and that His advice comes from wisdom and His position, as the one who is seated in the heavenlies and sees our situations from every possible angle. He wants us to wield the powerful weapon of obedience to defeat the enemy. As the apostle Paul wrote:

> *And you were dead in your trespasses and sins, in which you formerly walked according to the course of this world, according to the prince of the power of the air, of the spirit that is now working in the sons of disobedience* (Ephesians 2:1-2 NASB).

According to this verse, we live in trespasses and sin when we walk in obedience to the prince of the power of the air (which is walking in disobedience to God). This means that the opposite is also true. When we walk in obedience to God, we find freedom from the voices that try to draw us into sin. The choice is ours. So many of us live with pain and consequences that spring from our choice to believe and act upon the voices that lie to us. They shout things like: "Don't trust"; "They don't want me here"; "I'm not worthy to be loved"; "Everyone always rejects me"; "That's not fair"; and so forth. It is so easy to believe these lies and to act based on those beliefs—but that is disobedience to God. The truth is that

God is a good father, that He loves us very much, and that we are safe in Him.

I believe these voices that we give place to originate, as Ephesians 6 tells us, from powers, principalities, and rulers:

> *Finally, be strong in the Lord and in the strength of His might. Put on the full armor of God, so that you will be able to stand firm against the schemes of the devil. For our struggle is not against flesh and blood, but against the rulers, against the powers, against the world forces of this darkness, against the spiritual forces of wickedness in the heavenly places* (Ephesians 6:10-12 NASB).

The enemy's voice feeds us these lies. He never stops broadcasting, because he is the "prince of the power of the air," and he finds it easy to influence the sons and daughters of disobedience, the people who do not have divine life flowing in them. He finds it easy to convince them that they deserve a break, that they need to look out for Number One (because nobody else will), and that anxiety and stress are just part of normal life.

Without much effort, the prince of the power of the air can also woo us into believing that the Christian life is based on a fairy tale and that God's love is puny, not strong. The enemy's repertoire of lies is just about endless. Even if we capture all of his lies as they run through our minds, and even when we have the appropriate truth with which to counter each one, we can become exhausted in this continuous struggle to break free. The enemy's lies are so pervasive in the human condition, in culture, and even in the Church that we often find it difficult to discern them as the lies they truly are.

LEARNING THE ART OF OBEDIENCE

Unfortunately, even when we discern truth, it doesn't always lead instantly to obedience. I have to daily remember that God is good, that He is for me, and that He is working all things for my good. These truths allow obedience to flow more easily from my heart, enabling me to daily choose agreement with His ways rather than fearing the "swat!" Yet, even with this determination, it can still be hard to wholeheartedly embrace the idea of obedience, as many of us understand it.

Our trouble is that the very words *obedience, obey,* and *submission* carry a lot of baggage. Lots of red-blooded, independent-thinking Americans object to anything that smacks of caving in to somebody else's authority. We tend toward extremes when we approach the topic.

There's the over-spiritual extreme: "Oh, Dawna, don't worry about me. God and I, we're like *this*," as the person intertwines two fingers in the sign of intimacy. "No one has to tell me what to do or that I am doing anything wrong, because I hear directly from God. It's all good. I always follow His voice, even if *you* don't think it's Him talking to me."

Then there's the once-a-victim-now-independent extreme: "You don't understand, Dawna. Obedience has not been safe for me. I have lived under abusive parents, bad teachers, and cruel bosses. I can't trust anyone. I'm good on my own, thank you."

If it is true that the only way we can turn off the enemy's voice is by being children of obedience, then that is probably why the enemy has worked overtime to harm our relationships with those whom we are supposed to obey. He has seemed to work overtime to make those relationships toxic so that we will be leery of all obedience, even to God. Remember, I am not saying that we should always obey indiscriminately. I am saying that we *will* end up pledging our allegiance somewhere and that the enemy wants to keep us from surrendering it to God. I find it very interesting that Ephesians 6:10-12, which shows us the schemes of the powers of the air, comes right after these verses on obedience:

Children, obey your parents in the Lord, for this is right. Honor your father and mother (which is the first commandment with a promise), so that it may be well with you, and that you may live long on the earth. Fathers, do not provoke your children to anger, but bring them up in the discipline and instruction of the Lord. Slaves, be obedient to those who are your masters according to the flesh, with fear and trembling, in the sincerity of your heart, as to Christ; not by way of eyeservice, as men-pleasers, but as slaves of Christ, doing the will of God from the heart. With good will render service, as to the Lord, and not to men, knowing that whatever good thing each one does, this he will receive back from the Lord, whether slave or free. And masters, do the same things to them, and give up threatening, knowing that both their Master and yours is in heaven, and there is no partiality with Him (Ephesians 6:1-9 NASB).

The enemy, you see, does not want us to learn how to obey at all. He knows that if we learn to obey God, we will become familiar with His voice, and we will start to turn off the enemy's lying voice. Jesus said, *"My sheep hear My voice, and I know them, and they follow Me; and I give eternal life to them, and they will never perish; and no one will snatch them out of My hand"* (John 10:27-28 NASB). We want to become fine-tuned to *His voice* first and foremost so that we will recognize His Spirit when He speaks through the voices of human leaders.

THE TRUTH SETS US FREE

Most of us have lived long enough to make friends with something ungodly. We all have some secret sin that we do not know how to get rid of until God's Spirit shows us what to do—we obey Him. However, we can become pretty skilled at explaining these sins as something besides disobedience, and it can be hard for us to want to give them up. Take my experience as an example. As I grew up, I had so much energy that I would run around, do sports, and work hard, but then I'd become exhausted, and I would crash for most of a day, just sleeping. I loved it. I still love sleeping, and I so look forward to taking naps while all wrapped up in a nice warm blanket.

However, over the years, in my sleep-time world, I learned that dreaming could be really fun. In fact, I learned that I could manipulate my dreams in order to live out any adventure I wanted to conjure up. Who needed to pay for a movie? I could just lay my head down, and any storyline I wanted would come to life. I did not think there was anything wrong with this. It was just using my imagination. And boy did I have a great one! When I became a Christian, I Christianized these dreams. I made a special effort not to fantasize about sexual stuff or anything unChristian. In fact, I was the hero who always helped people. In my dreams, I would be the prophetic voice for the police force who would help find lost children. I would be like James Bond and Wonder Woman rolled into one, standing for justice and kicking the enemy's behind. It was great!

But over the years, it became more than a dream. These false realities began calling to me—wooing me to find rest and peace in them. For example, if I had a bad day at work and came home to find that my kids were squabbling, I could go to bed and forget all about my less-than-perfect life. In my dreams, I would be beautiful and amazing—all night long, and I could escape the drudgery of my ordinary life.

One day, just a few years ago, I was telling a friend about this. She said, "Dawna, I can't do that."

I thought, Bummer for you. Then you must have a pretty boring time when you sleep.

But that wasn't what she meant. She looked at me and said, "Dawna, that is the spirit of fantasy. You're listening to its voice, and when you do that, it keeps you from hearing God's voice."

Uh-oh, could she be right? And if so, what am I going to do? This spirit of fantasy had been with me for most of my life, and it had been a lot of fun! It didn't care that I was insignificant in real life; it actually probably pointed that fact out to me several times a day so that I would come and seek peace with it in my dreams. But simultaneously, it worked to rob me of God dreams and God's ability to bring peace to all circumstances, not by me running away from them, but by staying present and bringing His truth into my waking reality.

The spirit of obedience helped me to conquer this spirit of fantasy, and I know that it will do the same for you. Learning to walk safely in obedience will set you free from your need of any "old friend" that brings you comfort outside of God Himself. There are no limits to our freedom! Here is how it worked: At night, when I laid my head on my pillow and felt my old friend calling to me, I began to take hold of those invitations, and I took them straight to Jesus. I quoted to myself the truth from Scripture:

> *We demolish arguments and every pretension that sets*
> *itself up against the knowledge of God, and we take*
> *captive every thought to make it obedient to Christ*
> (2 Corinthians 10:5).

Then the spirit of fantasy would talk to me louder and begin pointing out the harshness of my day, telling me, "Come away. Let's be amazing tonight!"

And I would say back to it, "I am determined to be a child of obedience. I will not go away with you, and I invite You, Father God, to send your Spirit to comfort me—to take out the pain of life, to heal all bitterness and hopelessness inside...."

I won't lie, some days were better than others. Some nights were much harder to win. And sometimes, I would give in to the seduction of the false comfort and begin to intentionally dream away. But the more I confronted the spirit of fantasy's voice and allowed God to heal my discouragement and disappointments, the quieter and quieter it became—to the point that it hardly talks to me at all anymore. I think it has found out that unless something really big has occurred in my day, bothering me is now a waste of its time. On my worst days, that voice still tries to woo me away, and it really can be tempting, because I have missed those dreams. But I say right out loud before I go to bed, "I am a child of obedience, and I am choosing to turn off your voice, and I close any door to your power."

Sometimes God can set a person free in a "swoosh," and that person will never be the same again. I know we have all experienced such deliverance and are so grateful for those times because the other kind of freedom requires some follow-through on our part. He breaks us free and exposes the lies we have believed, and then He allows us to walk out our freedom, step by step. He wants us to really relate to Him—neither to obey our own instincts, which may well be faulty, nor to obey a set of rules ("Do not taste. Do not touch. Do not think."). And He wants us to *grow up!* I am convinced that He is less interested in my comfort than in my relationship with Him. But as I take all my discomfort to Him, He picks me up, wipes me off, and whispers His secrets to my heart.

I know it sounds like this is all about self-determination, which you will need, but it goes without saying that He is the One who shows us our false obedience in the first place. That's called *conviction,* and it comes with the grace to turn away from the old friend in order to follow your New Friend more completely. Are you ready to allow the Holy Spirit to be your comfort, to allow Jesus to be your true friend? Are you ready to trust that God is for you, not against you? Then ask Him to show you your "old friend."

If you ask Him right now to show you an old friend, don't be surprised if He does. He might use another person to tell you, or He might show you outright what to call this thing. After you have a name for it, you can repent of it. You can say something like this, inserting what He has shown you (anger, despair, fear, etc.) in place of "old friend":

> *Holy Spirit, I repent. You are my true Comforter, and I have pushed you aside and let other voices do Your job. Today, I stand as a child of obedience, and I choose to follow You, Holy Spirit. I choose to follow my Father God and Jesus. Through the shed blood of Jesus and in His name, I break covenant with this (old friend)—and I mean business.*

Then you can address your old friend directly, like this:

> *(Old friend), if you have been generational, if you have wooed my family, I'm fighting not just for myself, but also for my children, my grandchildren, and their children to come. I'm telling you that as I win this, your voice will not be able to draw my family any longer, and I command you off my family line!*

Turning back to God:

> *Father God, I hand over to you this "old friend." I also hand you my sorrow and grief and my sense of loss in turning my back to this known false comfort. I ask Your presence to be so near to me that, as this "old friend" continues to beckon me, You will overwhelm me in such a way that I will no longer thirst for its voice. Grant me the grace, Father God, to take my thoughts captive as I fight as a child of obedience. Thank you, Father, that we are going to break the power of its voice for good.*
>
> *Come, Holy Spirit, and comfort me as I fight this battleground of my mind, and remind me, Holy Spirit, to put on*

the full armor of God so that when I have done all in my determination to stand, You, Holy Spirit, will release to me the grace to stand!

Amen!

Chapter 3

SMOOTH BUT DEADLY

Beni Johnson

SOMETIMES WE JUST HAVE TO take charge! One night when I was sleeping, I had a horrible nightmare that woke me up. It totally freaked me out, and Bill was out of town. I tried to go back to sleep, but every time I would finally doze off, it would just come right back again. I struggled through the night because it never stopped coming back.

The next night, I remember walking toward my bed, thinking, *I do not want to do that again,* but inside I knew it was probably going to happen all over again, and it did. But this time, when the nightmare came, I woke up *mad*. I got out of bed and said, "Whatever is in this room, whatever is on my bed, you had better get out! You do not belong here anymore!" And the thing left for good.

You know how it is when somebody tries to harm a child and the child's mother just roars into action: "Nobody's going to hurt my baby!" Even if the situation is a very scary one, nothing is going to stop her. In the same way, no matter what threatens us, we have courage on our side. Sometimes, it is just up to us to get aggressive.

ORDINARY BECOMES EXTRAORDINARY

Because of the way it illustrates courage, one particular Old Testament story has recently become one of my favorites. At first it starts out to be a story about Deborah and Barak, but it ends up being a story about a woman named Jael. Most of us are familiar with the passage that we find in the fourth chapter of the Book of Judges.

The Israelites had been conquered by Jabin, the king of Canaan. For twenty years, he had oppressed them severely. The commander of Jabin's army was named Sisera. The commander of the Israelite army was Barak, who seemed to lack the courage he needed. Then Deborah (and later Jael) joined the fray:

> *Now Deborah, a prophetess, the wife of Lappidoth, judged Israel at that time. She sat under the palm tree of Deborah between Ramah and Bethel in the hill country of Ephraim, and the Israelites came up to her for judgment.*

> *And she sent and called Barak son of Abinoam from Kedesh in Naphtali and said to him, Has not the Lord, the God of Israel, commanded [you], Go, gather your men at Mount Tabor, taking 10,000 men from the tribes of Naphtali and Zebulun? And I will draw out Sisera, the general of Jabin's army, to meet you at the river Kishon with his chariots and his multitude, and I will deliver him into your hand?*

> *And Barak said to her, If you will go with me, then I will go; but if you will not go with me, I will not go.*

And she said, I will surely go with you; nevertheless, the trip you take will not be for your glory, for the Lord will sell Sisera into the hand of a woman. And Deborah arose and went with Barak to Kedesh....

And Deborah said to Barak, Up! For this is the day when the Lord has given Sisera into your hand. Is not the Lord gone out before you? So Barak went down from Mount Tabor with 10,000 men following him. And the Lord confused and terrified Sisera and all his chariot drivers and all his army before Barak with the sword. And Sisera alighted from his chariot and fled on foot. But Barak pursued after the chariots and the army to Harosheth-hagoiim, and all the army of Sisera fell by the sword; not a man was left.

But Sisera fled on foot to the tent of Jael, the wife of Heber the Kenite, for there was peace between Jabin the king of Hazor and the house of Heber the Kenite. And Jael went out to meet Sisera and said to him, Turn aside, my lord, turn aside to me; have no fear. So he turned aside to her into the tent, and she covered him with a rug.

And he said to her, Give me, I pray you, a little water to drink for I am thirsty. And she opened a skin of milk and gave him a drink and covered him. And he said to her, Stand at the door of the tent, and if any man comes and asks you, Is there any man here? Tell him, No.

But Jael, Heber's wife, took a tent pin and a hammer in her hand and went softly to him and drove the pin through his temple and into the ground; for he was in a deep sleep from weariness. So he died.

*And behold, as Barak pursued Sisera, Jael came out
to meet him and said to him, Come, and I will show
you the man you seek. And when he came into her tent,
behold, Sisera lay dead, and the tent pin was in his tem-
ples. So God subdued on that day Jabin king of Canaan
before the Israelites* (Judges 4:4-9,14-23 AMP).

I find it so interesting that Jael gave Sisera milk, which repre-
sents hospitality. Jael was really smooth. She welcomed the enemy
commander into her tent and made him feel safe by offering to hide
him and provide for him. She treated him with extraordinary kindness—before she killed him with extraordinary courage. We do not
know anything about her except that she was Heber's wife; the Bible
does not give us any more details about her life. But if she was a
typical wife in that culture, she was "just a housewife." We do not
know if she had children, but I'm sure she probably did. I envision
her spending all of her time taking care of her husband and her children, in and around their tents, wherever they made camp.

And yet when it came down to doing what God wanted her to
do, this ordinary housewife became this courageous woman who
could lure her enemy into a trap and then kill him singlehandedly
while he was sleeping. She acted hospitably toward Sisera on the
surface, but underneath she was exasperated. The severe oppression
of the Canaanites had gone on long enough. If Barak couldn't or
wouldn't take Sisera out, she would do the job. Just as Deborah
had prophesied, an ordinary woman—not the seasoned military
commander of 10,000 troops—got the glory for defeating the
Canaanite army.

Sometimes we just need to get angry like that—not at the people, but at the injustices and the works of the enemy! That is what
I call righteous anger, and it can be the key motivation in helping
us to partner with the Lord in specific circumstances and situations
that He has placed us in.

COURAGE COMES FROM THE HEART

None of us were equipped with courage from birth; we need to practice it. As you may know, the root of the word *courage* is *cor*, which is the Latin word for "heart." *Courage* is about putting your heart in a vulnerable place. All of us need courage, not only when we need to handle things that threaten us physically, but also when we need to contend with mental, emotional, and spiritual opponents. We especially need courage in order to break off all kinds of fear. "Breaking off fear" simply means no longer partnering with fearful thoughts. Fearful thinking is toxic thinking. There are other kinds of toxic thoughts, too, and as they fill our minds and replace our good and faith-building thoughts, they will zap our courage away.

The New Testament uses the word *courage* often and shows us that God wants us to *take* courage—to take hold of hopeful and courage-building thoughts and to take action accordingly. Here are a few examples, with the word *courage* highlighted:

> *And when they had prayed, the place in which they were assembled was shaken; and they were all filled with the Holy Spirit, and they continued to speak the Word of God with freedom and boldness and **courage*** (Acts 4:31 AMP).

> *Because of our faith in Him, we dare to have the boldness (**courage** and confidence) of free access (an unreserved approach to God with freedom and without fear)* (Ephesians 3:12 AMP).

> *When the disciples saw him walking on the lake, they were terrified. "It's a ghost," they said, and cried out in fear. But Jesus immediately said to them: "Take **courage**! It is I. Don't be afraid"* (Matthew 14:26-27).

> *But Jesus turning and seeing her said, "Daughter, take* **courage***; your faith has made you well." At once the woman was made well* (Matthew 9:22 NASB).

I am not prepared to judge a person's lack of courage too harshly, but if we take the words of Revelation literally, they might motivate us to work on our courage:

> *But as for the cowards and the ignoble and the contempt-ible and the cravenly lacking in courage and the cowardly submissive, and as for the unbelieving and faithless, and as for the depraved and defiled with abominations, and as for murderers and the lewd and adulterous and the practicers of magic arts and the idolaters (those who give supreme devotion to anyone or anything other than God) and all liars (those who knowingly convey untruth by word or deed)—[all of these shall have] their part in the lake that blazes with fire and brimstone. This is the second death* (Revelation 21:8 AMP).

We can practice courage by paying attention to our thought lives. When fearful or toxic thoughts cross our minds, we can heed our hearts (our spirit, which is in touch with God's Spirit) when they nudge us. It's like our hearts are saying, "Um, I don't think you should listen to that thought, because if you do, it's going to poison your mind and then you'll react out of that thought."

We must listen to our hearts. They will enable us to take cour-age so that we can boot out the poisonous thoughts and move on. This is Scriptural—taking our thoughts captive. I like the way *The Message* Bible puts it:

> *We use our powerful God-tools for...fitting every loose thought and emotion and impulse into the structure of life shaped by Christ. Our tools are ready at hand for clearing the ground of every obstruction and building*

lives of obedience into maturity (2 Corinthians 10:5-6 MSG).

Breaking off our partnerships with toxic thoughts and fears and courageously partnering with faith instead will bring us into maturity and peace.

ANGELS ON OUR SIDE

I would be the first person to say that I need plenty of outside help to confront the circumstances of my life with courage and resolve. Especially when I'm on my own, I need the ministry of angels. We sometimes forget about them because we do not sense or see them very often, yet God's angels stand alert and ready to fight off evil on our behalf. We cannot boss them around, but we can ask God to release them into a situation. Even just talking about them and remembering what they do can stir them up.

When Bill is not home, and I am home alone, I often turn the stereo on really loud. One day, I was getting ready to leave the house, and I started to go over and turn off the worship music. All of a sudden, I got this distinct impression: *No, leave the stereo on because the angels will really like it on after you are gone.* It was a random thought that just came into my head. So I thought, *Oh! Okay!* and I realized, *They are having a party without me.*

Angels bring the Kingdom. They bring the presence of Jesus. They are messengers, and they do His work and His work only. I also believe, based on the story we read in Acts 12, that each one of us must have an angel that looks like we do:

> *Peter knocked at the outer entrance, and a servant named Rhoda came to answer the door. When she recognized Peter's voice, she was so overjoyed she ran back without opening it and exclaimed, "Peter is at the door!"*

"You're out of your mind," they told her. When she kept insisting that it was so, they said, "It must be his angel" (Acts 12:13-15).

Angels come in a wide variety of sizes and types. There are healing angels. There are seraphim, the fire angels. There are cherubim, the wind angels, which are my favorite ones. Some appear gigantic to us, while others appear to be very small or like shadows.

Certain angels seem to carry particular characteristics so that people can identify them. One of our granddaughters had an infection when she was born, and she ended up in the NICU (Neonatal Intensive Care Unit) at the local hospital. Her mother (our "daughter-in-love") was there with her, and one night, she saw an angel standing in the corner of the NICU with his arms folded, just watching. She said he looked like Mr. Clean.

Eight years later, another grandchild was born; our daughter had a little baby boy. He had an infection and he too was cared for in the same NICU for many days, as his cousin had been. One night Bill was there with our daughter, and they were just visiting with each other, sitting by the baby. All of a sudden, Bill said, "I see an angel in here."

And our daughter said, "I know; I see it, too."

He asked her, "Does it look like Mr. Clean?"

"Yeah, it does," she responded.

Both babies recovered, and we knew that the "Mr. Clean" angel had been watching and protecting them. Mr. Clean seemed to be a watchful, caretaking angel. Maybe there is more than one of them. Likewise, once when I visited Mahesh and Bonnie Chavda in North Carolina, they shared with me that many years ago when their son was born they saw an angel just like that in their NICU. They said they still see that angel at their prayer watches every Friday night. He just stands there with his arms folded, watching and protecting.

Whatever their disposition or appearance, angels are always diligent at their work. In their emotional structure, clearly they are not the same as humans. Have you ever heard of a weeping, depressed angel? That's because Heaven is full of joy. I don't think they are as intuitive as we are, either. They can carry messages and follow orders, but they don't create the messages or the orders. In my experience, they are one-track-minded, and they can get frustrated to the point of complaint when they cannot do their assignment.

Along the same lines, they cannot read our emotions very well, although they can distinguish our level of faith and our realm of authority. Somebody once told me that angels can't comprehend our unbelief. They just don't get it. How could one of His creatures not believe in God and His Kingdom?

Obviously angels have great access to God and to Kingdom power, but they occupy a lower place than we do. They do not call God "Father." They do not preach the Gospel. Those are two things that humans do. And since they are not prophets, they seem to need to hear the word of God as it comes through their fellow messengers, humans.

Angels help us in warfare, to the point that they sometimes carry all of the warfare for us. I had an experience in this regard. Bill and I had been in Australia, and I was coming home by myself earlier than he was. My flight from Sydney got canceled, so I had to spend the night in a hotel room near the airport. This sort of thing was starting to become normal for me, and the other times it had ended up being a God thing. So I expected God to use it somehow.

That evening, I was online chatting with a friend who lives in Hawaii. I went to bed praying for her, because her husband had just had some type of mental breakdown, and she was trying to get help for him. They were just a young couple, and it was a really difficult situation.

In the middle of the night, I heard a crackling sound in the room. I had heard this particular sound once not long before, when I was sharing a hotel room in Bakersfield, California, with my assistant. When I had heard it the first time, I had suspected that my assistant had gotten up to help herself to something from the snack basket. But when I had lifted up my head to see, my assistant was still sound asleep in her bed and I could see a dim form of a person or something over by the snack basket. I had not been scared at all; I just went back to sleep, because I knew it was an angel.

This time in Sydney, it felt different. I knew an angel—my angel—was in my room, but I also knew that there was a war going on in there. I knew it had to be because I had been interceding so much for this young man in Hawaii. There was fear in the room this time, and it was intense. But instantly I remembered that my angel is very big and very protective. So I thought, *Piece of cake. My angel's going to take care of this.* And I just went back to sleep. I actually kept my head on the pillow the whole time, and I never did look up, because I really did not want to see anything. In times like that, our angels come to do warfare for us.

With a greater awareness of angelic help, we can expect great things to happen. We can ask the Holy Spirit to release angelic activity for our neighborhood, our town, and the world. This is one of the surest ways of pushing aside the darkness.

YOU MAKE A DIFFERENCE

Hard times and obstacles will not disappear anytime soon, but we are not defenseless when we face them. Not only do we have God's presence, the strong help of the angelic host, and the sturdy courage that comes up out of our hearts, but we also have each other. You are not alone, even if you feel isolated and alone where you live. Ask God to send you somebody, a kindred spirit, with whom you can share honestly.

Ask God's Spirit to give you an idea—something specific that He wants you to do to release more of His strength and wisdom for you or for someone else. Very often, God-directed physical acts bring spiritual fortification.

Not long ago, a man was shot and killed by the police in our city. He was not a good man. In fact, he had been involved in illegal activities, and his death was not a big surprise. But when my intercessor friends began to come to me, each one sensing that something had been stirred up in the city, I knew I had to pay attention. I found out that the man who had been killed was a leader of a clan in the area and that they were very angry that he had been killed; they were planning to retaliate. Inside, I objected. *No you don't! Not on my watch! No, no, no. Not here!*

I had an idea, and I knew it came from God. I have a shofar, and I had not blown it for quite some time. In my experience, blowing the shofar is a good way to release peace over a region and also to cause confusion to the enemy's camp. So first I took one of my intercessor friends along with me to the site where the man had been killed. We prayed there. We repented for all the bloodshed that was over the land because of his killing. We prayed through the whole area, essentially arresting the evil spirits that must have been released when he died, spirits that I presume he was carrying because he was so angry and violent. Then I went to our house of prayer at sunset, and I blew the shofar and declared, "There will be peace over Redding."

I was simply standing on the authority that I have been given in prayer and not letting the atmosphere of fear and spiritual harassment get in the way of what God wanted to do. Each one of us has been given an arena of authority, and we will be expected to exercise it. For many, it's a family or a small group of people. For others, it's a larger region, a city council, or a department of government.

In order to exercise our authority, we need to learn how to identify the battleground and to use the appropriate tactics. We need to become adept at vanquishing the lies that the enemy inserts into our minds, and we need to be willing to step out into fearful situations with courage. (It's important to note that what may require courage for me may not be the same thing that requires courage for you.) We need to band together with others so that we are not isolated and vulnerable, but strengthened together and always aware that angelic assistance is just a breath away.

Are we willing and ready for more? If we all do our part, the Kingdom will come more quickly. We can repeat these familiar words with passion: *"Your will be done, on earth as it is in heaven..."* (Matt. 6:10).

Chapter 4

ALL OF HEAVEN IS
CELEBRATING YOU

Theresa Dedmon

MEMORIES ARE THE CRADLE OF life's greatest treasures. Inside your attic or mothball closet, stashed away in hope chests or boxes in the garage, you will find them. Photographs of when you or your children were young, the first paintings that hung on your fridge, crumpled Christmas decorations with glue stuck everywhere but where it was supposed to be—you scavenge through memories of yourself and the people you love. In such moments, you find the first inklings of what all of us celebrate and value in life—each other.

Our hearts reveal what we celebrate. As women, we hold these memories dear, dreaming of what the future will hold for those we love. I can just picture Mary, the mother of Jesus, putting Jesus' first carved toy in her hope chest. In that split second, she undoubtedly pondered all the prophetic words about her son, the Messiah. And later, because she *knew* His destiny, she was able to draw on her relationship with Him as a mom, asking her son, Jesus, to perform His first recorded miracle—turning the water into wine for the wedding guests (see John 2:1-11). I find it interesting that Jesus was influenced to reveal His destiny through His relationship with the one whom He appeared to treasure the most. Maybe moms *do* know what's best. He honored His mother's request, and thus, the party was epic! Jesus revealed Himself as the King of kings at a wedding with friends and family—all because mom said so. (Snapshot time!) Women have an incredible influence in changing the course of history.

This chapter is about finding out how the King of kings wants to celebrate you as a woman and reveal to the world who you were created to be! Every time He sees you, all of His dreams come flooding in to give you hope for your present and future. If you look closely enough, you can see Him watching you now. He has the heavenly version of the iPhone—probably the Infinity brand—and His camera is pointed at you! It's time to get your party hat on and come to the never-ending celebration of God's goodness and love, which He desires to lavish on you.

This may appear strange to you, so let's look at what Papa God thinks.

> *How precious are your thoughts about me, O God. They cannot be numbered. I can't even count them; they outnumber the grains of sand. And when I wake up, you are still with me* (Psalm 139:17-18 NLT).

Wow! Have you ever gone to the beach and picked up a handful of sand? It would take you hours just to count that small handful. Imagine just how powerful His intentional love and favor is for you right now—like numbering the expanse of sand, it's beyond your comprehension. This truth needs to radically shift the way you view yourself and your worth. God's thoughts of you continually are washing over you like the waves of the sea, crashing against any other thought or imagination that is not in alignment with His goodness. Every time you see the seashore, remember He is thinking thoughts about you and celebrating *you!*

UGLY COMPARISON

Let's take a look at what most women think about who they are. Sadly, a lot of women view their femininity and worth as inferior when they look at the magazine advertisements for lingerie or makeup. They have been taught to compare themselves by looking at who they are not—rather than who they *are*. This makes a woman hide her worth and true beauty, disguising the greatness of how she was uniquely designed by God. I don't need to tell you the stories of countless women who are in counseling, suffering from self-hatred or emotional scars, because they have felt less than or inferior. Why does this happen? Deep down, most of our culture has been impacted by comparisons in our looks, personality, and worth. Many of us have tried to cover it up with a smile or have bought into the lie that if we just go on this diet or take this class, then we will feel okay inside. Many times we are afraid to admit the devastation we feel inside about how we look, our personality, or the way we feel in a crowd of people.

Women can also feel useless, unwanted, or insecure in the Church realm because, many times, the Church has defined their role by what women *cannot* do, rather than who they are in God's eyes. Again, this leads to confusion and lack of clarity. A big question for many has been, "Is a woman allowed to preach, minister, or teach in a church setting?" Even if women are allowed to preach in church, are they actually given the opportunity to do so, or is it simply token theology without any evidence? This sort of contradiction between belief and action is another source of insecurity for many women in the Church. Although we celebrate female heroes in our churches, many times they are from past eras or are living far away from the church we attend. God celebrates your value in the Body of Christ, and He wants your dreams for being significant brought into the Body of Christ so that every facet of His Body can be celebrated and revealed. Let's take a look at what Jesus thinks about us as women.

KNOW *WHO* YOU ARE

When I was in Bible College, I was looking for role models to follow as an emerging woman leader in the Church. I asked a woman whose husband was a professor at the university where I attended if she would disciple me and meet with me. I will never forget her response. She began to share her belief that a woman should lay down her personal dreams for her husband's vocation. This meant that I was supposed to sacrifice my pursuits if they interfered with my husband's schooling or ministry experience. Based on her assessment, coupled with my naiveté, I decided never to meet with her again and never to open up my dreams to other women in the Church who might put me down for even having them. I made a promise to myself at that time that if I got the chance, I would disciple women to fulfill their call and never make them feel like second-class citizens—like I had felt. Every person has a right to a dream and to be valued. Each one of us has the right to pursue who we are meant to be.

God qualifies us in the Body by *who* we are to Him, and He doesn't compare us to others: *"There is neither Jew nor Greek, slave nor free, male nor female, for you are all one in Christ Jesus"* (Gal. 3:28). I am blessed to be part of a movement that celebrates women and gives them permission to happen, and you are also a part of this new breed! All women have something of worth to add to the Body of Christ. Now is the time to learn to celebrate what you can offer to others in the Body of Christ. Now is the time to free yourself from thinking about what you cannot do in church and to find out what you *can* do.

Hundreds of people in your city are waiting for you to find out who you are through Christ's eyes; they need you to teach them and bring transformation to their lives through your heart for God and the Body of Christ. Take some time this week and be a blessing to someone in your church, some woman who has been working there for years, but doesn't know how valuable she is. Make a change by blessing and calling out the treasure inside of her. If you start with what you have and bless women along the way, you will create God's goodness for women in your church. Don't let what is not happening in the Body of Christ be the news that gets published, but what *is* worth broadcasting ignored.

I have good news for you: the way God sees you and made you matters *more* than any thought that you've had or comparison that you or others have made about you or your value as a woman. God wants to turn the muddied waters of our minds and culture into the supernatural wine of the Spirit, just as He did at the wedding of Cana. Women are anointed and empowered, and we have been given permission by Jesus, who holds all authority, to live and be free from comparison or "less than" thinking.

> *So from now on we regard no one from a worldly point of view. Though we once regarded Christ in this way, we do so no longer. Therefore, if anyone is in Christ, he is a new creation; the old has gone, the new is here* (2 Corinthians 5:16-17).

Nothing disqualifies you from who you are except the way you perceive yourself apart from God. Esther was just a beautiful maiden until she won the heart of the king and saved the Jewish nation. I have Good News—you have that same privilege and position with the King of all kings! Instead of looking at our limitations or constraints, let's focus on what we *do* have! We have Jesus' approval, and that's all we need to redeem the value of every woman alive!

Moses was a man who had a burden to set God's people free, but through circumstances, his anger at the Egyptians cost the life of an Egyptian; thus, he was exiled for forty years. You would think, at that point, that it was over, but God's thoughts for Moses were catching up with him in the desert sands. All of a sudden, he was granted His desire, but sadly, he began to compare himself to others. "God, I stutter. I can't talk eloquently, but what about my brother, Aaron?" God completely ignored him, saying that I AM would be with him (see Exod. 3). You see, God's Word changes everything. Moses was concerned about what he *was not,* but God not only knew who *he was,* but also that His Presence would go with him. This makes all the difference in the world.

ACCESS TO THE FATHER'S HEART

When I was fresh out of Bible college, the pastors at the church I was attending asked me to head up the women's ministry and counseling at our Vineyard church. In the back of my mind, I was already disqualifying myself. *I'm not funny, like my husband, Kevin. Who am I to lead all these things? They should get a person who is more experienced!* What saved me from missing out on this opportunity was asking God's opinion about it. He told me that if I needed Him that much, I would be the best leader for the position. His perspective changed everything. I was looking at what I lacked, when He was looking at my connection to Him. If you are connected to God, every thought He has is sending a blessing to your heavenly bank account, where you have the green light to withdraw whatever you need. Why? Daughters have access to their Father's heart!

In retrospect, I see that because I listened to God's voice, I have had the privilege of pastoring people ever since I was twenty years of age, and I have been involved in many moves of the Spirit, leading women's studies, retreats, and programs. In my years of pastoring, I have found that one of the most common choices that will abort a woman's life purpose is learning to live under a curse that has already been broken. Jesus has paid the price so that every woman can live in abundance, be blessed in her femininity, and explore how God has uniquely designed her. Women have not only been loosed, but they have been empowered to live out their dreams. Everywhere, God is raising up champions who will empower women to fulfill their potential as royal daughters who are free to pursue their dreams, both within and outside the Church.

So many women have subconsciously agreed with the wrong spirit and have thought that they were limited as women. Right now, I want you to make a stand and cross over to the resurrected life that Jesus promised for every believer. All pain, depression, fear, worry, insecurity, and rejection have no power against the blood of Jesus that was shed for you. *You are His happy thought!* He is the way, the truth, and the life (see John 14:6), and He has provided all you need *and desire* to walk into your destiny!

THE SIGNIFICANCE OF YOUR DREAMS

Another wrong mindset that God wants to change for women is the belief that their dreams are secondary or not important to God. I am not just talking about dreams that are attached to saving the world, but personal dreams as well. This may be unfamiliar territory, but it's true! God has designed *every* part of your life to prosper. If you have a dream, it's important to Him because you are His child. You, like many women, may have never felt like you had liberty or permission to explore how God created you to be in every area of your life. God has given you permission!

Personally, I believed this worldview; it was so integral to the fabric of my thinking that I didn't know it until I came to Bethel Church in 2002. You see, I thought God was interested in what I could *do for Him* in ministry, and I had not explored other facets of what I love in regard to the other passions in my life. I had subconsciously believed that these were not as important and that they were not worth pursuing. However, through prophetic words given to me after I came to Bethel, God awakened me to embrace all of who I am in my passion, giftings, and call. I was born in a highly creative and prophetic home, but I had laid that down because I thought it wasn't relevant to God or in ministry. I was in love with Jesus and wanted to do everything I could to serve Him. So instead of taking an art scholarship to college, I went to Bible college. This was fine, but the lie that this decision was founded on was that God's dream for me didn't include my passions, experience, and desires. I had separated part of who I was from all that God wanted me to be.

I even had a vision that I share in my book, *Born to Create,* the first Sunday I was at Bethel. In the vision, I was painting in the back of the sanctuary while Pastor Bill Johnson, our senior pastor at Bethel, was preaching. I remember how embarrassed I was and how I tried to hide what I was doing behind some chairs so that I wouldn't be the focus or interrupt what Pastor Bill was saying. A year later, I realized that God had been speaking to me similarly to the way He had spoken to Peter in Acts 10, when he saw the vision of the unclean animals coming down from Heaven and finally began to understand the inclusion of the Gentiles in Christ's plan for redemption. In the same way, I could not understand God's desires to bless me in the things that I loved. I hadn't understood that this was important to Him—just as important as ministry or preaching. Wow, did I get a revelation bump! God *really* wants you to know that He created *you* to experience His pleasure and blessing in every area of your life. God wants us to be integrated and to have every part of our lives blessed. Not only that, but also our ability to minister to others will be found as we reflect *all* of who we are. Now, I partner with the Holy Spirit, creating art that brings encounters and healing to others all around the planet. God never intended to give us gifts that He would not bless.

Not only has God anointed me and poured out His abundance on me in all areas of my life, but He has also fulfilled my dreams for allowing creativity to flow not only through me, but also through others who have never before given themselves permission to create or dream. I have had the honor of leading in Bethel's School of Supernatural Ministry (BSSM) for the last eight years, and I have now transitioned into overseeing all of the Creative Arts at Bethel and BSSM. Now I travel around the world, sharing with people that God has designed them with a creative DNA, which they can explore and activate. In other words, every one of us reflects a different facet of God's creative design because we are made in His image. If we try to copy others or compare ourselves to others, the world and the Body of Christ will never *see* a certain facet of God that we alone carry. So woman of God—be set free to explore every facet of who you are without fear of failure, wondering if what you're doing is important to God.

I want you to know today, as you read this chapter, that God wants to release you from skewed thinking about your worth. He made you as a woman and gave you talents and calling, and He wants to bless every part of who you are. You are *valuable to Him as a person*, not just as a project or a way to see others get saved. He loves everything about you and wants to hear your dreams today. So what are your dreams? Tell Him right now! What are the things that you have buried deep in your heart? Let Him know. As you release them to Him, He will be your champion and bring others to you who can help you succeed. Not only will this impact you, but it will release dreams in your children and your children's children! Imagine what your scrapbooks might be full of if your daughters and granddaughters catch a vision of who they are because they saw their mom and grandma live out her dreams! Your dreams are not just tied to your destiny, but to the destinies of those you love dearly. Remember the hope chest and the faded ornaments, and get busy believing in God's abundance. If you forget, go ahead and start counting the sands on the seashore!

BE EMPOWERED!

We as women need a revolution of belief about ourselves in our personal lives, but the Church as a whole also needs a revelation of the value God places on women and who we are destined to be in the Church. Now is the time! God wants to set the Church free to empower women of all ages. Not long ago, I had an experience that illustrates this perfectly.

I was leading a CREATE Supernaturally conference at a church when one of my dancers asked a young girl to dance in worship with her. Sadly, this young child said that her father had forbidden her to dance in church. My dancer, Saara Taina, pleaded with her to ask her father again, as he had seen our dancing team release many in their church to dance that weekend. So she went to ask and returned running to Saara, clasping her hands together, and squealing, "Yes! My daddy said yes!" In the same way, your Daddy in Heaven has given you permission to dance, sing, write, paint, teach, lead, and be *all* that you were created to be. It doesn't matter how many "No's" you have heard; your heavenly Father says "Yes!"

As a woman, I have a heart to raise up other women and see them grow in their identity, being fully released to understand their destiny. To this end, when I was co-leading Bethel's School of Supernatural Ministry, I would put on an event for all of our second year student women that we called our "Princess Party." My friends, Ron and Sue McDonald, would help me put on the most lavish five-course meal, where we would have music and festivities just to honor the women. We would create an ambiance that reflected God's heart and pray a blessing over them as women in revival. All of them would dress up, and many times we would buy tiaras or give them special gifts to train them in the extravagance of their worth to God and to the Body of Christ. Honor begets honor. The men in the school would also dress up and serve the women, waiting on them and making them feel like queens.

Such princess parties are a powerful demonstration of how God thinks about women, and they are easily replicated. Not only can you do this for women in your church or in your life, but you can also let the King of kings honor you and lavish His attention on you! When I was in high school, I would often prepare a meal during which Jesus and I would just sit down and talk. In other words, I saw myself as valuable and as worthy of His undivided attention.

God wants to celebrate you; He wants you to know that all of Heaven applauds you—the way you are uniquely made and what you carry. Go ahead and get out your camera and take a picture of the place setting, the beautiful china, the soft music playing off in the distance. You sip your drink outside in Heaven's lush garden and then the most wonderful smells fill your nostrils—delights from Heaven come before you. This feast is served not just for your children or family or friends—but this is in *your honor!*

IMPACTING THE NATIONS

Not only have I been able to bless the women in the school of ministry, but I also have a heart to transform the nations. After I put on a Supernatural School of Creativity week at Bethel, I ended it with a festival called Heart4Nations, where I helped raise awareness for all of the children in Africa. We had different kinds of booths that people could go to: food vendors, live entertainment, a dream interpretation booth, and prophetic art stations where people could receive a picture about who they are. We also had a booth where women could get makeup, a haircut, and a photograph of themselves—all portraying who they are. We had arts and crafts for children, as well as dramas, dances, and music interlaced through-out this event.

All of the proceeds went to help Heidi Baker, as well as other agencies that are helping children in Africa. We did this because I am a woman who loves children, and women who help them are important to me. My creative passions and my heart for revival around the nations can impact the world and those whom I love. Let's take another snapshot!

How can you, as a woman, with your unique passions and desires, impact the nations? Here is what I have discovered. As I travel to other nations, I am astounded at how many women need to know who they are and how valuable they are to God. My heart is to also reach out as a woman of faith to be a prophetic voice of encouragement and love. For the past three years, I have led mission trips to the Philippines. There I have had the privilege of seeing a mighty revival, where God is raising up an army of Filipinos who know their destiny. They are now taking supernatural creativity around the world and are seeing people get saved, set free, healed, and discipled. I call them my sons and daughters, and I am commit-ted to seeing them become all that they can be.

This is how I have begun to impact the nations, but obviously, the places and passions in my heart are probably different than yours. What nation do you burn for? How can you bring your gifts and strengths to transform that place? Take a snapshot of the coun-try you want to see touched by God, and ask God to release and empower you to be a mother there. Then watch and see how God will open up doors.

One very important vision that our hearts need to burn for is the many women around the globe who are living in slavery and bondage. We need to let their voices be known and to ask for a way to end their suffering. I am not sure how this will happen, but I know that God will partner my heart with His plans to end the sex slave trade and to see God's presence invade every dark area where women are treated as less than they truly are. Why do I believe this? Because they are my daughters, my sisters, and my mothers. So I pray, *God open the way!* I recently was able to paint a picture about the sex slave trade, which someone bought to help fund the ending of the sex slave trade. Let's be women of passion and action. Ask the Holy Spirit what your part is in seeing every woman freed so that she can run the sands of God's goodness through the palms of her hands over and over again.

Many times we need to ask ourselves the question, *"What if* I saw myself as God sees me? How would my life be changed? How would my relationships be different?"* Right now, let everything go and let the *what if* become the reality in your life.

Your Father in Heaven takes snapshots of you—the first time you created something without fear of performance or being perfect, the first time you loved yourself enough to pursue your dreams, the first time you took a step into your destiny. He doesn't care if it's perfect; He just cares that it's *you!* God is celebrating you right now! All of Heaven is saying "Yes!" to your dreams and to what you alone are designed to be! So put on your party hat, and let's take a picture!

Chapter 5

Keeping It Real

Jenn Johnson

Speaking Up

MOST OF US ARE REALLY good at encouragement. When we see good things in other people's lives, for the most part, we do a great job pointing it out. Social networking makes it especially easy. This is important, but it's only one side of friendship. True friendship means seeing and praising the good in our friends, and it also means challenging them on the hard stuff. I believe the Lord is inviting us into a place with each other where we are not only accountable for the good in each other's lives, but also for the weaknesses. We need to be encouragers, and we also need to be transparent enough to say what we really think.

Let's be real. No one is perfect. Stuff happens, and people fail—people who are really amazing Christians. No one wakes up one day and just decides to be a murder or adulterer. It's a slow, hidden process over time, a process made up of small choices that eventually create a lot of damage. This is where good friends come in. Often, we have the ability to see or sense that something's not right. And if we have the courage to talk to a friend when we see destructive patterns, we may help that friend get out of the mess before it explodes.

However, too often, when a person falls into sin, I hear other Christians—friends of this person—say, "I knew it. I saw that coming." That is wrong. The truth is, God allows us to see "what's coming" in people's lives so that we can speak up about it. Once we see it, we're called into the realm of accountability. And if we just sit back and watch, if we refuse to speak up when we see that something's wrong, we will be accountable. I'm not talking about gossiping to our other friends, but going to this struggling friend and telling her what we see. That's what Jesus said we should do.

> If a fellow believer hurts you, go and tell him—work it out between the two of you. If he listens, you've made a friend. If he won't listen take one or two others along so that the presence of witnesses will keep things honest, and try again. If he still won't listen, tell the church. If he won't listen to the church, you'll have to start over from scratch, confront him with the need for repentance and offer again God's forgiving love (Matthew 18:15-17 MSG).

Here Jesus clearly tells us that if we are dealing with an offense or a hurt, we need to go tell that person. In that place of confrontation in love, we can find healing. It is so easy to think we're being super-spiritual if, when we feel these emotions—hurt, betrayal, jealousy, resentment, and so forth—we say, *I'll just take it to the Lord.* Most of the time, however, we say this because of our fear or our pride. We don't want to admit what's going on. It's true that God is all powerful, and He is able to take care of our pain for us. However, that's not what Jesus said to do. He didn't say, "When you have an offense toward your friend, just pray about it, and I will take it away." Instead, He said, "Go talk to that person." He wants us to resolve our struggles together.

If I cut my arm badly and the wound is deep enough that I can see the bone, I would have two choices. I could put a nice flesh-colored Band-Aid on it and try to go on living as though it wasn't affecting me. Or I could get medical help. I could let the doctor clean the wound and put in stitches. The astringent and stitches will hurt—probably more than I realize—but afterward, the wound will be able to heal. However, if I choose the Band-Aid, not only will the wound keep hurting, but it will eventually get infected and bring pain and sickness to the rest of my body.

When it comes to emotional wounds, many of us choose the Band-Aid because it seems less painful and looks prettier at the start. We think, *I don't need to talk about what I'm going through. I can just deal with it with the Lord.* A Band-Aid is not a long-term solution. We all have emotions; we all experience pain in our relationships and feelings that get out of alignment. And we need to be real about it so that we can deal with it and move on. Or we need friends who will confront us and say, "Hey, you smell funny. What are you hiding under that Band-Aid, sister?"

GETTING ALONG

As a mom, I live tough love on a daily basis, and it is because I have goals for my kids. I expect them to grow up into amazing people who can love others well and who will change the world. On a day-to-day basis, however, usually my goal is just for my kids to get along. Our two girls are nine and six, and our son is four. They are amazing kids, but they spend a lot of time fighting. Some days, I feel like, *For real? Could you just get along for five seconds? I'll pay you a dollar for ten minutes of no fighting!* As a good mom, I love my kids, and I want to see them mature to the place where they can be kind to each other.

I think God feels the same way about us. My highest intentions and greatest love for my kids don't even compare to what God feels and thinks toward us. He has such incredible dreams for us, yet sometimes I wonder if He spends most days thinking, *Could you just get along? Could you love each other and be nice? Could you stop saying those words toward that other person, please?* He wants us to learn to love each other in real ways.

As I walk my kids through learning how to get along, just as God does with us, one of my biggest desires for them is that they learn and grow in their relationships to where they do not need to bring all of their disagreements to me. I want them to learn to work it out on their own. That's God's desire for us as well, and that's why we can't just take our troubles to Him and no one else. He wants us to mature to the point where we don't run to Him to resolve it (or run to our other friends to blab about it), but instead work out our disagreements together in love.

Obviously, this doesn't mean we should not talk to God about our struggles with each other. I'm not saying that He doesn't want to hear about it, but that He wants us to recognize our own ability to resolve conflict in relationships in a healthy way. In fact, when we are dealing with our feelings toward another person, it's crucial that we hear from the Lord about the appropriate steps to take care of the issue. If jealously is the problem, going to that person and saying, "I'm really dealing with jealousy toward you" isn't a good idea. Each situation needs a unique response, and perhaps one reason why we sometimes run from these tough love conversations is because we just don't know what to say. But God knows, and He wants to empower us with His wisdom so we can deal with the situation maturely.

An important part of this maturity is not blabbing what's going on to our other friends. We want to talk about it; that's natural. And we need to process, but that should be done with the Lord and, if we need another person to talk to, with a momma. A momma is not just an older woman, but one who has spiritual wisdom, one who's not just going to sympathize with us, but challenge us with the truth. If we are willing to humble ourselves and ask for help, we will always find a momma who can give us the wisdom we need. When issues come up in my life, this is what I do. I call a momma and say, "This is what I'm dealing with. What would you do? I need help." It's humbling, but I do it all the time because I know I can't do it on my own.

Many of us women are very strong. We do so much for our children and our families; we have the right answers for their problems. And it's easy for us to start believing we can do it all on our own. Because we are strong, we find it hard to ask for help. We think, *I'm an adult. I can do this, and I don't need anyone's help.* The first day I felt like an adult was the day I hosted my entire family for Thanksgiving at my house. I felt like, *I am an adult. I have arrived.* But the tricky thing about maturity is that we never really arrive, we never grow up so much that we don't need help anymore. Many of us think that needing help is a sign of immaturity—so we don't ask; we try to do it on our own. The truth is, recognizing our need for help and being willing to ask for it is a sign of maturity.

My husband, Brian, and I have been married for twelve years, and we go to marriage counseling every year. We just know that no matter how good our marriage is, we still need help. It takes humility, though, because some people do judge us for getting help. They're the ones sitting outside the counselor's door, watching the people go in and smugly thinking, *Oh, I knew it. I knew it.* Those are the sort of people we become when we refuse to ask for help. Eventually, we start judging everyone else. We think, *Well, I can do it on my own. I am so much more mature.* And we keep trying to believe this lie until our world falls in around us. The truth is that none of us can do it on our own. Instead, we should be applauding each other for getting help when we're going through something difficult. We should be cheering each other on as we take the risk of transparency.

TRANSPARENCY

This is not just true when we have personal offenses, but in all areas of our lives. We're all going to, at times, make poor choices that could potentially lead to big messes. Even when we're living holy lives, sometimes we just get "slimed," and in those moments, we need to run to Jesus—and we need to run to our friends. We are not supposed to just take it to the Lord. We also need to have a sisterhood in place—a safe place where we love each other with more than just encouragement. It's called tough love—meaning, "I love you, so if you're having a hard time and I can tell, I'm going to ask you about it. I'm going to pry because I love you too much to leave you alone in your stuff."

Some people don't want anyone prying into their issues. They like to quote *"Judge not, that ye be not judged"* (Matt. 7:1 KJV). But there's a big difference between judgment and tough love. Love doesn't always feel nice, but it always has our best in mind. God's tough love is called conviction—when He says, "You can't do that because it's not in My will for your life. It's not good for you." He doesn't force us to listen, but He doesn't make it easy for us to ignore Him, either. This is what we need to be for each other.

God does not intend us to live life connected only to Him. Sometimes, He will only speak to us through other people because He wants us to live in intimacy with Him and with each other. I experienced this when Brian and I were praying about whether to have more children. We have three amazing kids, and after our third was born, we both felt like we were done. But we were waiting for confirmation, to make sure that we were done because God wanted us to be done and not just because of what we wanted. One day we were out with some friends, who have four children, and the husband asked if we were going to have more. I told him where we were at, and he looked at me and simply said, "Three's a great number." When he did, I felt liquid peace go through my body, and I saw a picture in my mind of a big book closing. In that moment, I knew that we were really done and that it was God's plan. That was the confirmation I needed, and God gave it to me through a friend because we're a Body and we all need each other.

Transparency can be hard, but it is really important. First John 1:7 says, "*...If we walk in the light, as he is in the light, we have fellowship with one another, and the blood of Jesus, his Son, purifies us from all sin.*" Walking in the light means being transparent, letting people see into us—both the good and the bad. When we do that, according to this verse, not only will we be connected to the Body, but we will get free. We are purified by Jesus' blood as we share transparently about our stuff with one another. We like to think we can just take it to Jesus, but here again He is telling us that we need to be open and get help from our brothers and sisters, too.

If we could understand the value of being in the light, of being transparent and talking through our issues, we would stop harboring bitterness and letting wounds fester in our hearts. If we could see God's heart on this, we would live differently. We would see that healing comes through intimacy, through transparent relationships where we confess our sins and our struggles to each other (see James 5:16). Sadly, so many leaders have risen to a place of prominence, and because they thought they needed to do it on their own and they did not understand the importance of transparency, they fell hard. It is time for us to start preaching the value of transparency in the Church, to start training people to talk about their emotions instead of hiding them and trying to overcome them on their own.

How I Almost Lost My Heart

I understand the value of transparency because I have seen its fruit in my life. It saved our marriage and our ministry. About eight years ago, Brian and I were traveling and leading worship all over the place, and we were very busy. God had been speaking to me about slowing down, but I didn't want to hear that. I was running really fast, connecting with everyone I met, and just having an amazing time. In the midst of all the busyness, I formed a heart connection with another guy. He really understood me, and he was around a lot when Brian was busy. This guy didn't have a lot of responsibilities; he had time to talk and listen, to fill my quality time love tank.

My husband, Brian, is amazing, and this wasn't his problem, but mine. I loved him so much, and I still do, and I was not looking for another relationship, but in the busyness, I didn't guard my heart like I should have. And this connection formed. I didn't sin in this, but I felt connected. That sort of feeling is the beginning of a sneaky, slippery slope that can eventually cause a woman to wake up one morning and say, "I'm going to leave my husband and join this other man because he gets me." This is why the small choices in the heart are so important—and why transparency can save us from awful messes.

I was at the beginning of a potentially awful mess. This other guy was a wonderful guy, and he was not intending to connect with me or trying to fill some void in me. He was just being a great person. And one day while we were on a trip, I felt my heart go out toward him. He didn't know what was happening, but I saw it and felt it. All the frustrations and the lack that I had been feeling had suddenly found a place to be met—in this man who was not my husband. In the spirit, I saw my heart go toward him, and I ended the conversation right there. "I need to go," I said, and I quickly braced my heart, like I would put a broken arm in a cast.

Fortunately, all this happened right before our last session of worship before we went home. Before we led worship, I went behind the stage and cried out, "God, I'm in some hot water with this, and I need help!" I could have told Brian—wrecking his world and sliming the other guy in the process—but I knew I needed to just brace my heart until I could get some help. That night we flew home, and I literally called Danny Silk, who was Bethel's Family Life pastor at the time, from the airport. I told him I needed to talk to him, and then I drove straight to the church. I told him everything, and he lovingly talked me through putting my heart back into my chest.

Danny held his hands together, with his fingers intertwined like when a couple holds hands, and he said, "In a marriage, you're connected like this. Then as you go about your day and deal with the business of life, you slowly become not so connected." He pulled his hands and fingers apart until his fingertips were just touching. "What you have is the opportunity to catch it right here and reconnect," Danny continued. It was an invitation to rebuild that connection instead of catching it, but not really paying attention to it and letting it slip until the connection broke.

Eventually, Danny brought Brian in and, without going into exactly what was going on, we talked about what I was missing and why I was reaching out for something else. And we made it right. Through being transparent, not only was I able to restore the connection with Brian, but I was able to address the root issues in my heart, as well. I learned a lot. I learned about maintaining my connection with Brian and prioritizing him above my kids and above our ministry. It can be hard to juggle life, but God has the perfect schedule for each one of us. As Kris Vallotton once said to me, "There's enough grace to get done everything that you need to get done."

When I sat with Danny in his office and told him what was going on in my heart, I had to face my need to make some things right in my life. I needed to make better choices and do a better job of voicing my needs. Danny helped me to stop blaming people and situations for what did or didn't happen, and he helped me to reverse it. He taught me to say, "I feel" and "I need." It was humbling having to admit, "I have needs, and here they are." But it worked. We poured astringent on the wounds, and it hurt. I'm a strong woman, and I've been through a lot, but this hurt like hell. In the end, with Danny's help, I closed up that wound in my heart, and now I don't even have a scar.

We all face these issues in our lives, these moments when toxic emotions try to take over. We want to hide them, to put a Band-Aid on and hope they'll just go away on their own. But if we don't deal with the cut, if we don't bring it into the light and let others help us pour astringent on it, it will get infected. It will poison us. Thank God that, through transparency in the Body, there is another way. You don't have to sit in your stuff; just flush it.

GUARD YOUR HEART

In Proverbs it says, *"Guard your heart above all else for it determines the course of your life"* (Prov. 4:23 NLT). It says "above all else" because guarding your heart is really important. When you are going through something or a friend is going through something—you have two choices, two possible scenarios. You can ignore it, or you can confront it. Whether it's in your own life or your friend's, the choices are the same. I want to invite you to stop ignoring and to make the hard decision to confront the stuff that comes up in your life. And find a momma and get help. No matter how old you are, you still need help from other people.

I also want to invite you to address the pink elephant in the room in love. Nothing good comes from criticizing and gossiping about others, but a lot of good fruit comes from prayer. Care enough about your friends to ask about what's going on. Don't underestimate the power of your voice; don't forget the power that you carry as a daughter of the King. You are like Lucy, the little girl in *The Chronicles of Narnia,* walking next to the powerful lion Aslan. When something seems too big, too far beyond your control, remember that you are a little girl walking beside a big lion. He will help you as you confront the issues before you. You are not alone. There is incredible power in the partnership of a little girl and a lion.

Chapter 6

The Priority of Connection

Sheri Silk and Brittney Serpell

WHEN WE LOOK AT OUR lives, according to the big picture, we see that what really matters is the relationships we have—our connection with our heavenly Father, with our husbands, with our children, with our parents, with our siblings, and with our friends. These relationships should be our top priorities—and they are also the container for revival. In order to make an impact in this world and bring Heaven to earth, we need to have strong, healthy families. To have strong and healthy families, we need to learn to operate in love and to prioritize connection.

I (Sheri) recently met a man who did a survey at MTV, asking the MTV crowd, "What do you want help with in your life? What's the one thing that you wish you had help with?" The number one answer was, "I want a better relationship with my parents." This man went back to the MTV producers and said, "You guys don't even know your own audience. You're pumping them full of a bunch of garbage and giving them all this stuff, and what they want is relationship with their parents." We all long for that connection. Unfortunately, as this man's survey of the MTV crowd shows, many of our families and churches suffer from broken relationships. These relationships aren't broken because we just don't care about the people in our lives (or they don't care about us), but because so often our relationships are established on rules and control rather than on love and connection.

Several years ago, our family learned about the priority of connection in a very real way.

BRITT'S STORY

When I (Brittney) was sixteen years old, we had just moved from Weaverville, California, to Redding, California, and I was struggling with loneliness. I found myself in an Internet chat room with a boy who was returning some affection in a form that I had never known before. I had never had a boyfriend, and I found myself chatting away with this boy and loving the attention. Late night phone calls turned into planning a time to meet. The week before we decided to meet, our family was in Los Angeles, and I told my cousin what I was going to do. He was the only one who knew.

When the day came, I told my mom that I was going to a party at a friend's house, which gave me a reason to be gone all day. I then went and met this boy at a park. My mom, at some point during the day, was trying to get a hold of me, but she couldn't find me. She called the friend's house where I was supposed to be, and they told her, "Brittney never showed up." At that moment, her heart sank into the pit of her stomach, and she began thinking of all the bad things that could be happening.

As she was trying to figure out where I was, she remembered that my cousin and I had spent a lot of time together the week before. She called him, figuring he might know. He confessed and told her I was planning on meeting a boy I had met online at a park.

But he didn't know which one we'd decided on, and there are over twenty parks in Redding.

My mom was unable to get a hold of my dad because he was working out of town that day and was without cell phone service. She was home alone, and my dad and I had our only two cars. My mom was now spinning, thinking, *I don't know where my daughter is! What if something happens to her? I don't even know if she will be alive when I find her!*

In the meantime, I was having a good old time. My mom eventually called Kris and Kathy Vallotton, some of the only people we knew in town, and told them what was going on. Kris and Kathy prayed, and the Lord showed them exactly where I was. They drove right to me. I had been gone for about eight hours when they found me in the dark, kissing some boy I had just met.

Kris talked to the boy, and I called home, noticing that I had over forty missed calls. My dad answered and told me, through his tears, that he had just been describing to the police what I looked like. In that moment, I experienced a twinge of the pain of *Oh gosh, what did I just do?!* But I couldn't deal with that thought because I was sixteen and I thought I knew it all, so I decided to be mad instead. I geared up for a fight.

While Kris and Kathy talked to my parents, I sat and waited for my punishment. I had my boxing gloves on and was ready to go. They came in the room, and in my mom's eyes, I saw anger because being scared looks like anger. My dad was calm, and I thought, *He's probably in shock.* As we began talking, my mom and I were butting heads. Then my dad took over and started asking me questions like, "What were you doing? What were you thinking? What's going on? Why would you do this?"

I just spun in with, "You have no idea the pressure I have being your kid. I come down here, and I'm Danny Silk's kid. Everyone knows everything about me. I'm constantly being compared to my friends. That's the pressure I live with being your kid, and I hate it! I don't even know if I want to be a Christian anymore."

In response, my dad crawled across the floor, put his face and hands on my knees, and said, "Britt, I will give it up today. I will quit my job being a pastor. I will go back to being a social worker because my goal at the end of this is that you, your mom, and your brothers are all on the other side. That's all I care about. If it's too much pressure for you, me being a pastor, I will stop today!"

My dad emphasized the fact that his relationship with me was way more important than anything he could ever do for a living, more important than where we lived or what he did for a job. At that moment, I started to realize I was the priority in their lives. My parents both continued to love me and show me that our connection was their priority, and within the span of several months, I realized how much I had hurt them. I walked away from those bad choices and the bad boyfriend, and I chose relationship with my parents and with God instead.[1]

ANGER IS FAKE POWER

This situation was very scary and painful for Danny and me (Sheri), but we knew that protecting and strengthening our connection with Britt was more important than anything. While Britt was trying to figure out her life, we tried not to muddy the process of her journey with anger. If we had added anger and lots of rules to the equation, that's what she would have been looking at. She would not have been open to what God was doing because she would have reacted to our anger by pointing her anger at us. And she certainly would not have felt our love.

Anger is fake power. It makes you feel powerful, and it makes you feel like you're in control of some things. However, the truth is that none of us has control over anyone but ourselves. On a really good day, I control me. On a really, really good day, I control me all day long. I tell myself what to do, and I do it. Unfortunately, we have this illusion with our children (and sometimes with other people, too) that we can control them. When they're little, we can actually pick them up and move them. There is a sense of control in that, but as they get older, controlling our kids is a joke. We cannot do it. We can if they choose to be compliant, but if they choose not to be compliant, we find out pretty quickly who is in control of who.

When we're confronted with situations and relationships that feel out of our control, we often respond in anger because it makes us feel powerful. But it is an illusion. It makes us look scary and powerful, and sometimes it makes people move. It seems to work—especially when our kids are little. However, if we treat our kids like this when they're little, many of them, once they hit the teen years, will start to give it back. They will realize that the relationship has become about who has the power and that anger is the medium for that power, and they will show us how incredibly angry they can be.

Anger is *very* disrespectful, yet so many of us sow it, over and over, into our relationships with our kids, with our husbands, and with other people. We massage it into the soil of our relationships, and eventually our kids grow up and other people get fed up, and they start giving it back to us. We may think, *What happened? Who is this rebellious teen? What happened to my husband?* The reality is, it's harvest day, and we're reaping what we've sown. We've used anger to get power in our relationships, because feeling a sense of control is our priority. In return, we get relationships that are based on control, not on real connection and love.

BLINDED BY FEAR

When relationships are tested, many of us also respond in fear. Fear and anger are closely connected. We are terrified by the reality that someone we love deeply could deeply hurt us. Thus, when we see our child or husband or friend do something that scares us, we go a little bit crazy. We do not act like ourselves when we are scared.

When I was twelve years old, I went swimming in a lake with my cousin, who is two years older than me. We were both great swimmers, and I was even on the swim team. I had no problems swimming. We were standing up in water that was deep, but not over our heads, and we were playing. Then, all of a sudden, we stepped off of a ledge. We didn't realize there was a drop-off in the lake, and it scared us. Even though we were great swimmers, we began floundering in the water as if someone was holding us under. We could both swim, but we were freaked out, and we were literally taking turns dunking each other, trying to get back up on the ledge. Eventually, my uncle had to dive into the water fully dressed and pull us up to where we could stand.

It was ridiculous, and it illustrates what happens to us when we are afraid. We stop acting like ourselves, and we start attacking anyone nearby. All we care about in such moments is self-preservation. When Britt ran off with the boy, I was terrified. I had no idea where she was or what might be happening to her. I was facing the possibility of very big pain in my life, and it scared me like crazy. When we found her and she was okay, that fear threatened to come between us. The fear wanted me to do whatever was necessary to protect my heart and prevent Britt from hurting me like that ever again. So many of us respond this way in difficult and painful situations. We are scared of being hurt, so we stop acting like our normal selves, and we start reacting out of a desire for self-preservation.

However, fear makes it impossible for us to show love to others. We need to deal with our fears and determine to love, no matter what happens. As a mother, I've had to face the fact that it's quite possible that the very ones whom I brought into the world may hurt me more than anyone else on the planet—and I've had to decide that, no matter what, I'm going to love big.

CONNECT WITH THE HEART

Once, I talked to a mom in England who was having a lot of trouble with her fifteen-year-old son. She told me that he was sneaking out of the house, had gauged his ears and gotten a Mohawk, and was hanging out with bad kids. I tried giving her some suggestions, but she kept saying, "That won't work." She was hurting because she loved her son so much, and she was struggling to maintain hope. Moms have such incredible love for their children; it's powerful when it's pointed in the right direction!

So I looked at that mom, and I said, "I think you should look past all of your kid's behavior and find that little boy's heart that you knew when he was a child. Go in and try to touch his heart. Don't look at his Mohawk. Don't look at his ears. Don't look at his outfit. Don't look at his friends. Don't look at any of that stuff. Just go in and try to connect with that kid's heart."

During the days following the crisis with Britt, it felt like we were in a black hole. I felt completely disconnected from her because she was doing her best to not connect with us. We can try to connect with someone, but if that person doesn't want to connect with us, what can we do? We just kept loving her. We refused to give up, and we kept our love on. In the midst of feeling so distant from and hurt by Britt, Danny and I knew that our relationship with her was paramount. If we didn't have that, what else mattered? So we did all we could to protect and strengthen that connection, even though it didn't seem very strong, even though she didn't seem to care. No matter what she said or did, we kept our love at the forefront. And eventually love won.

STRENGTHENING THE CONNECTION

In the end, all we have is our connections with people. Those connections can be made out of a kite string or a steel fishing line strong enough to catch a shark. We decide what the ropes that connect us to others are made of. If we want strong ropes, if we want shark-catching steel lines, we need to prioritize our connections with people as being more important than the details of the conflict. Only when the connections are strong will we be able to successfully put pressure on the relationship without destroying it.

If I try to confront you about something that is really hard or painful for me when our connection is a kite string, it won't turn out so well. If I've only invested enough love into our relationship to build an easily broken string, then I have not invested enough. When conflict comes, the connection will break. However, if I have done a really great job of investing in our relationship and making it a priority, when I come to you and say, "Hey, when you do this, it really hurt me," I have something to pull on. The relationship is strong enough, like a steel fishing line, to hold the tension and weight of conflict. When we have a strong connection like that, when I pull on the relationship, you will be able to hear my heart when I pull. You will want to stay connected to me because I've made an investment that is worth something, that is heavy, that can handle the tough spots. Before we confront another person, we need to know what our connection with that person looks like.

If we realize that we are disconnected from a person—our child, our spouse, or anyone—our biggest priority must be to reconnect. Our priority must not be addressing and fixing the problem. That will just destroy the already weak relationship. Instead, we should not even look at the problem, and we definitely should not talk about it. The most important thing is the connection, and until we have the connection, no real solution to the problem will exist. Any solution that's found without connection is a solution that wounds the other person and further weakens the relationship. Instead, we must find the point of disconnect. We must remember back through the relationship to the point where the connection suffered—perhaps a conflict, an external pressure, an internal struggle, or something in the environment. Once we find the break, we must begin to intentionally strengthen the connection in that place.

I like to imagine our relationships as bridges between people. Our relationships are what connect us, what enable us to get into each other's hearts and have a genuine love exchange. So when we evaluate our relationships, we can ask, "What is the bridge between me and that other person made of? Is it a concrete, stable bridge, or is it a wobbly, falling-apart bridge? If there was a big cliff below and alligators in the water, would I walk on this bridge?" These questions can help us have perspective, can give us an image for what we're attempting on an emotional and relational level. If we wouldn't walk on that bridge in real life, we should not risk it in our relationships either.

Yet so many of us venture out on these weak connections because we have strong emotions about our situation. We think, *I'm angry at you, and I'm going to confront you and tell you what's up.* And we find ourselves standing on the creaky bridge that can't hold all this conflict, and we begin to fall. Suddenly, our problems get much bigger. Now we need to deal with other issues, with the alligators in the water below—things like drinking and driving, teenage pregnancies, affairs, betrayal, and other ultra-painful situations. When we violate the strength of the bridges between us and other people, we opt for pain. Because we have violated the other person in this way, that person will work hard to keep a distance from us. Sometimes the other person will even try really hard to hurt us. Ultimately, it turns into a cycle of striving for control through hurting and intimidating the other person—and all genuine connection is lost. Though we may not always realize it, this is what many of our relationships have become because we have not prioritized the connection above anything else.

With our kids, the connection is especially vital. Most of them are not mature enough to reach out and connect with us if we have not first connected with them. That's our job as the parents. Danny often talks about our kids as kites. Each kite has a string, which is the relationship the parents have with that child. It can be made out of steel, or it can be made out of cloth. We are holding the string, and as our kids grow into teenagers, the wind begins to blow. People are influencing them; people we don't even know are speaking into their lives. And so they fly amid the swirl of friends and teachers and coaches and celebrities—the many voices with many opinions—and the only thing we have is our connection with them, our kite string. The stronger our connection, the more weight our voices will carry and the more stability we'll be able to lend to their journey.

That picture is pretty scary for us as parents; it's full of realities and possibilities that we can't control. And the truth is that sometimes it doesn't matter what we do. We can have very strong connections with our kids, yet at the end of the day, they still get to make their own choices. That's the privilege that freedom gives them, and as a result, they may end up in a tree somewhere. It doesn't matter. We just need to keep the relationship on, no matter what. All relationships have pitfalls because we are imperfect people. We try our best, but we still make mistakes. So even when we invest in our connection with our kids, it is still possible for them to blow away like a kite on the wind. It just happens. Relationships don't have a fail-proof formula. The key is to not let the mistakes and the rough patches derail our love.

LOVE WINS

I have often heard Bill Johnson say, "Rules without a relationship equals rebellion." So many parents major on the rules and prioritize obedience over relationship. But the connection must always be most important. When it's not, we will reap rebellion. However, prioritizing the connection does not mean eliminating all rules, either. We have to have rules. During the months following Britt's choice to run off, we did not have to remove all rules in order to strengthen the connection. We let her date the boy, but it had to be on our terms and in our house. We had plenty of rules, but we made sure she knew that our relationship with her was way more important to us than the rules. Rules are necessary, but if we have *only* rules, we're headed for rebellion. We need relationship and connection first.

Psalm 32:8-9 says,

> *I will instruct you and teach you in the way you should go; I will counsel you with my loving eye on you. Do not be like the horse or the mule, which have no understanding but must be controlled by bit and bridle or they will not come to you.*

In this passage, God clearly shows us that He doesn't want us, as His children, to need a set of rules and instructions. He gave Israel the Law to show them the right way, but relationship has been His desire from the beginning. And over and over again, we see the pattern in the Old Testament that when the people were not connected to God's heart, they rebelled against Him. He wants us to fall in love with Him. He wants us to look Him in the eye—not the from-across-the-room, you're-in-trouble-again evil eye, but His loving eye. That is why Romans 2:4 says, "*...the kindness of God leads you to repentance*" (NASB). He's inviting us to look into His face and see how what we're doing is affecting Him. That's what developing a connection does for us. When we have that connection with people, they will care about how their choices affect us.

Stacy Westfall, a horse trainer and nationally recognized competitor in horsemanship events, has proven this point powerfully through what she has achieved with her horses. She has won multiple freestyle reining competitions while riding her horses with no saddle, no bit, and no bridle. She doesn't even use a neck rope. She simply guides the horse by love. From childhood, Stacy's mother taught her to try to understand what her horses were thinking and why they did what they did—to get inside their minds.[2] From that place of connection, she has been able to do amazing things, not through external controls, but through relationship. For example, horses don't like to gallop; they like to trot, but that is painful for the rider, especially with no saddle. Not only does Stacy get her horses to gallop, but she also gets them to go from a full gallop to a complete stop in just a few seconds—without a bit or bridle. Her horses also do figure 8s. This means that if the horse is running with his right foot forward, he'll switch leads and start running with his left foot forward. Her performances are an incredible display of the love relationship between a woman and a horse.

The way Stacy Westfall is able to lead her horses, without bit or bridle, to do what they wouldn't naturally want to do, demonstrates the power of prioritizing connection. Our relationships will be able to stand up under extreme pressure if we have invested in this level of connection. Like the horse who gallops and stops without external controls, we too will choose to do things we don't necessarily like to do because of how it affects those we love. And they will do the same for us because our relationship with one another has become our highest priority.

Endnotes

1. For a longer version of this story, see Brittney's dad's book, *Loving Our Kids on Purpose* by Danny Silk (Shippensburg, PA: Destiny Image, 2008).

2. "About Stacy Westfall," *Westfall Horsemanship;* www. westfallhorsemanship.com/content/meetus/ (accessed

April 6, 2012). A video of Stacy riding bareback and bridleless can be viewed at www.westfallhorsemanship. com/seeus/category/2/.

Chapter 7

Finding Adam

April LaFrance

Remember the story of Sleeping Beauty—the lovely maiden who was cursed to wait until her Prince came to rescue her with a kiss and whisk her off to Ever After? For years and years she slept, unable to move forward in life, trapped by her circumstances, all her hopes and dreams suspended, waiting for her Prince to arrive.

Sound a little too familiar?

It seems that far too many of us can identify with Sleeping Beauty's plight. We carry the dream of marriage in our hearts, we've done all of the "right things," and yet for some reason, it just doesn't seem to be happening. We're stuck waiting for God to make things happen, waiting for a man to finally come and knock on our door so that the dream can begin. And then the difficult questions beckon:

I feel like You made me for marriage, Lord, so why hasn't it happened yet? You've healed me and filled me, and I'm ready to share my life with someone. Actually, I've kind of been ready for a while now. Is there something wrong with the men around here? Or is there something wrong with me? Maybe it's You, God; is there something I've done or haven't done that's causing You to withhold a spouse from me? Well, anyway, I'm ready when You are. I'll just wait right here and listen for the knock on the door. Ready and waiting....

Many of us have prayed prayers like this. But what we need to realize is that there is a crucial difference between Sleeping Beauty and us. She was under a curse that froze her and prevented her from pursuing the love that her heart longed for, but we have a God who has rescued us, redeemed us, given us free will, and empowered us to make good choices. It's time for us to wake up to what our role might be in moving toward getting married and discover what it looks like to actively partner with God on this journey.

Most of us are comfortable pursuing the other dreams we have—dreams that have to do with our careers, our ministries, our hobbies, or our passions. But when it comes to the dream of marriage, we have an expectation that God will sovereignly "make it happen." In our minds, to actually *do* anything ourselves would be to tamper with "The Plan."

Imagine for a moment that God gave you a dream to become a medical doctor and work toward health and justice in a developing nation. You would probably begin by making a plan. Researching different universities, you'd prayerfully choose one, apply for it, and once accepted, begin your studies. After a few years of study, you'd do an internship, then a residency, and then start looking at gaining experience that would be helpful for you when you move overseas. The whole time, you would be partnering *with* God, while making strategic choices and moving forward toward the dream.

I'd like to suggest that there shouldn't be a difference in how we pursue and partner with God in our dream for marriage and in how we'd partner with Him in any other dream. Most of us would think it was crazy if someone's sole plan for achieving the dream of becoming a doctor was to wait and pray. And yet that's often what we do with our dream for marriage. It can sound really spiritual and almost heroic, the idea of *waiting for the one,* but in reality, most things in the Kingdom require us to act, to walk, and even to face challenges.

We'd all love to hear the audible voice of God telling us who to marry or to have someone literally arrive on our doorstep and sweep us off our feet. But that's not often how God leads His free people. It's possible, and we've all heard the stories, but in general, God has set up a model of partnership, where we co-labor with Him in our decision-making and where He expects us to take active steps toward the things that He's offering us.

I believe that it is God's intention to fulfill the desire that He put in our hearts for marriage. He only ever sets us up for success—which means that we were all made to live a love story. The question is, what does it look like to partner with God in pursuing the love story that He has for you? While everyone's journey is going to be different, there are definitely some practical steps that you can take to begin to work *with* God in pursuing this dream.

We're going to look at a few things—healthy dating, where the men are, and how to communicate with a potential guy, or what I like to call GGF (good girl flirting!).

DATING

Firstly, we need to learn what healthy dating looks like. Within the Christian community the word *dating* can have a lot of different meanings attached to it, and our own personal experiences will influence whether the word conjures up images of blissful romance or fear and dread! One thing that is really important to recognize is that dating doesn't mean that you've given up on God or that you're taking things into your own hands, and it certainly doesn't mean you're desperate. If you are at a place in life where you're ready to build a relationship for a lifetime, then spending time with someone, with the goal of finding the man you're going to get married to, is a healthy step to take. I'm not talking about recreational dating, which is when you date someone simply because he's cute and funny and makes you feel good, but rather when you date *on purpose* with the end goal of finding someone you can share your life with.

A DATE ISN'T DATING

Going on a date is not the same as dating someone. A "get-to-know-you date" doesn't have to be high pressure, and it's completely reasonable if you decide at the end of it that you're not interested in going out again. Going on a date is really just a way we've come to describe spending quality time with someone. Maybe you meet for coffee or dinner or hang out doing something together. Going on a date does not automatically qualify you for a level of commitment with a guy. And if either of you decide it's a no-go at the end, it doesn't mean you've made some kind of terrible mistake either. Here's some truth: It's almost impossible to know before you start spending time with someone if he's going to be compatible with you or fit the vision you're running with in your life, so getting to know him through a date or two is an essential part of the process.

A HEALTHY DATE

In First Timothy 5, Paul gives instruction on how to treat younger women. He says to treat them with purity as if they're your sisters. I think the concept is one we can apply to the beginning stages of dating. Brothers and sisters can have coffee together, they can eat food together, they can talk together, and they can enjoy each other's company. The greatest foundation of any romantic relationship is friendship. Keeping the brother/friend perspective at the forefront when building a new relationship can really help us guard our hearts from running ahead of our reality and creating unnecessary drama.

Most guys will agree that the less pressure women put on them in the beginning stage of the dating process, the better. Guys are actually often afraid of the pressure that women can place on them (an example of pressure would be you assuming that he wants to marry you simply because he asked you out for coffee). It is your responsibility to manage your own heart and expectations on a date and to recognize that the guy is just figuring out where he's at too, and he might not know by the end of one date. You need to be in a position where, at the end of a date, you can say to yourself, "I'm going to choose to give him the freedom to decide whether he wants to pursue more relationship or not, and I'm not going to disrespect him if this isn't a direction he wants to go."

Dating (in the Ongoing Sense)

Let's say you've been on several dates and spent a bit of time with someone, and you both decide that there is the potential in your relationship for it to grow into marriage; that's when you start defining your relationship as *dating*. Simply put, *dating* is two people choosing to commit to grow in friendship with the purpose of considering marriage, all the while resisting the urge to act like they're already married. Resisting the urge to act like you're married can be tough, especially if you're dating over a length of time. But the truth is that the person you're dating is not completely yours. In fact, he still could end up being someone else's, and you need to treat him with that in mind.

Invite Wisdom

Healthy dating invites wisdom and feedback. Pray about potential partners, and invite God's presence into all of your dates and relationships. It's also really important to ask for feedback from friends, leaders, and people you trust. Ask them questions like, "What do you think of this guy?" and "What do you think of our relationship? How do you think we work together?" Proverbs 11:14 (KJV) says, *"Where no counsel is, the people fall; but in the multitude of counselors there is safety."* It is so helpful to have the insight and discernment of others, and it makes the dating process much safer and healthier.

WHERE THE MEN ARE

Here's a fact that may shock you: Census research shows that there are more single Christian guys who have never been married than there are single Christian women who have never been married.[1] What may be a little less surprising, though, is that there are more women attending church than men.[2] So the truth is, good Christian men are out there; you just need to find them. It's time to learn how to not be hidden.

Go Where the Men Are

If your normal routine in life does not provide you with opportunity to regularly meet several potential guys, then you need to consider going where the guys are.

One effective way to meet more potential guys is to sign up for an ongoing class or activity that interests you and that has *a lot of men* in it. Now, you probably shouldn't crash the men's breakfast at your church, but a Kingdom Business class, a hiking group, or a volunteers meeting for an organization like Habitat for Humanity are all great places to meet new guys. And let's not forget golf! A golf course provides lots of potential for quality getting-to-know-you time, and generally the moustaches far outnumber the skirts on the golfing greens. All you have to do is start learning to play and then search for the churches that hold annual golf tournaments!

Enlist the Help of Some Friends

You want to get married right? Put the word out to some friends. Let people know what you want, and enlist their support. All you have to say is, "I want to be married to a great guy. Do you know anyone in my age range? Do you think you could introduce us?" You'll probably find that your married friends get especially excited about this and say that they've wanted to set you up for years anyway! Now, here's the side note: Don't ask anyone and everyone to be involved; just choose a couple of friends who you trust, and make sure that they follow through.

Use Your Resources

If you're not dating online, you should be. Research shows that one out of every five relationships right now begins online.[3] I recommend signing up for one mainstream integrous dating site and at least one specialized or niche dating site that is geared toward spirit-filled Christians. Our dating website, www.OnDaySix.com, was formed specifically to connect Kingdom-minded singles with integrity. OnDaySix also offers incredible video tutorials online to help educate you on how to choose a spouse and how to love the one you choose. If you're new to online dating, ask a friend to help you. It makes it much more fun and can help give you vision for a guy whom you might have passed by before.

Good Girl Flirting (GGF)

What do you do when you get around a good guy? Many single women have a track record of freezing up and ignoring guys they're interested in, making sure they look busy when that guy's around and hovering around in girl gangs for "protection." And they wonder why no one is asking them out. You need to learn how to give a guy "go" signals to indicate that you are open, friendly, warm, and potentially interested in being asked out. It's time to learn the artful skill of what I call *Good Girl Flirting!* This isn't flirting to boost your self-esteem, to get attention, or to see what kind of power you have to get a guy to respond; it's simply creating a safe space where a guy can be comfortable that you're going to respond to him in a friendly and open way.

Here are some tips:

1. *Make eye contact and smile at him.* This seems obvious, but some seem to avoid making eye contact if a guy happens to have any potential at all. All you need to do is look at him; then you look away; then you look back. If he's still looking, that's a really good sign! Open, friendly people are people who make lots of eye contact and smile.

2. *Hi, what's your name?* Men have way more anxiety about asking us out than we think they do, so why not simply say hello, ask his name, and be friendly. This is not aggressive, and this is not to be confused with you pursuing him. You are being friendly; he still needs to work to ask you out if he's interested.

3. *Touch him on the arm.* A lot of guys feel cared about through touch. I'm not referring to sexy touch; I'm talking about innocent touch. A touch on the arm while you're talking to him or emphasizing a point is a perfect way to demonstrate that you care and are interested.

4. *Acknowledge strength.* Affirm and respect him by telling him what he's good at. This doesn't need to be

weird, but can just come naturally in conversation. If he is telling you hunting stories and says, "I shot a 12-point buck," then you can respond by saying, "Wow, you must have a really good aim." When you do this, you're showing him that you're listening to him and you're acknowledging his strengths.

5. *Say his name.* Using someone's name makes that person feel known and cared about, so make sure you refer to him by name during conversation.

6. *Ask for help with something.* Don't act helpless, but ask for help with something. Guys like to feel needed, and they like to know they have something to offer, so find something that you need help with, and create an opportunity for him to be a hero!

7. *Ask open-ended questions.* Avoid asking him questions that can be answered with just the words *yes* or *no.* Instead, ask open-ended questions to enable him to share who he is and expand the conversation. "What do you think about..." "What do you like to do..." and so forth.

8. *Dress Modestly.* Keep modest in the way you're dressed. Men get super-distracted and find it hard to function when you put too much on display.

Now you may be wondering: *Can't I just be myself? Why do I need techniques to attract a guy?* In my opinion, sometimes it really isn't enough to just be authentic in sharing yourself. To be successful in dating or even in friendship, you need to think about how other people are interpreting you. Communication happens two ways. It's not only about what you give out for communication; a huge part is in how it's understood. Your intention in doing or saying something may be great, but if guys are interpreting it differently, then it's probably time to readjust the way you do things. A good way to gauge this is to ask your friends for feedback. Ask them how you're doing and how they think the guys around you are interpreting you—and then be open to adjusting the way that you behave.

I want to mention an important line between acting warmly and friendly toward relationship and being an aggressive husband-hunter. There's a huge difference. John Calvin once said, "The evil in our desire typically does not lie in what we want, but that we want it too much."[4] Marriage is a good thing, and God created a desire in most of us to want it, but it must not take center place in our hearts above God and other people. Ask yourself, honestly, whether you have the ability to respect someone who is not interested in dating you. You should be able to put such a person's best interest above your own and bless him, even when he doesn't pursue you. You can also ask some friends for feedback to make sure you're not communicating to the general public that you're on a man hunt. If you have been hunting, ask God to help you to find a healthy balance for your hope.

WHAT'S STOPPING YOU?

For most of us the biggest thing that stands between us and the discovery of a potential relationship is fear—fear of dating the "wrong" guy, fear of messing up God's plan, fear of making a poor decision, fear of ending up with a broken heart. But here's the thing: You are not alone in this journey. You have been given access to all wisdom through the Holy Spirit, and you are walking with God in every aspect of your life. Yes, there is risk involved when you move forward toward a dream, but some things in life are worth the risk. And love is one of them. A lifelong partnership with someone you love really is all that it's cracked up to be. It's worth fighting for. It's worth being brave for. It's worth boldly facing your fears to start partnering with God toward relationship.

My encouragement to you would be to awaken yourself to move forward with God in finding and building an incredible marriage. Use wisdom, and take courage. God is more than able to help restore you, guide you, lead you, and teach you as you partner with Him to see a God-given dream fulfilled. Yes, this still requires risk. But the greater loss would come if you let fear win by remaining asleep in the castle—waiting for a rescuer to come when, truly, your rescuer has already set you free.

MADE TO LIVE A LOVE STORY

A couple of years ago, God placed a vision in my heart. He gave me a glimpse of what it would look like to see a generation of the healthiest marriages that have ever walked the planet—couples who walk with God in power to advance the Kingdom of Heaven, who are passionate worshippers, and who *love* each other well. I have a vision for a generation of couples who reflect the goodness of God and are known by their remarkable *love*. The power and influence of that generation of Christian marriages will surely change history and astonish the earth for His glory.

I invite you to experience that kind of marriage—a marriage that reflects the absolute goodness of God and the power of covenant love, a marriage that brings restoration to God's original intent for marriage on the earth. Now is the time to ask God to bring His truth and vision into your particular circumstance; to lay down disappointments, unanswered questions, and pain from the past; and to let the Holy Spirit come and fill you with hope and anticipation for the good things to come. I am believing with you that as you begin to use these tools, as you let go of fear, and as you partner with God to pursue the dream of marriage, you will live your way into your very own real life love story.

Endnotes

1. Candace Watters, "Plenty of Men to Go Around, Part 1," *Boundless* (August 2006); http://www.boundless. org/2005/articles/a0001325.cfm (accessed May 3, 2012).

2. Ibid.

3. "Match.com and Chadwick Martin Bailey 2009-2010 Studies: Recent Trends: Online Dating" *Match.com* and *Chadwick Martin Bailey;* http://cp.match.com/cppp/ media/CMB_Study.pdf (accessed May 3, 2012).

4. John Calvin, quoted in C.J. Mahaney, "The Idol Factory," *ChristianLibrary.org* (Sovereign Grace Ministries, 2001); http://christianlibrary.org.au/cel/documents/ Idol%20Factory%20-%20C%20J%20Mahanoney.pdf (accessed May 3, 2012).

Chapter 8

Renewed Thinking: Overcoming Mood Disorders

Julie Winter

As a family nurse practitioner, I treat at least three patients daily for anxiety or depression, many of whom are Christians. There are numerous causes for mood disorders, and certainly the stressors in our society play a significant role as well. However, Christ lives in us, and we have access to the mind of Christ. Since the mind of Christ is full of peace, faith, joy, and love, this should be the state of our minds as well. I believe the normal emotional state of the believer is peace and joy. We cannot express Him accurately if we are anxious, sad, fearful, doubting, angry, or hopeless. For many, Christ living in us will be the only Christ the world will ever see. So it is important that we show the world what a renewed mind looks like. The purpose of this chapter is to outline some of the root sources of mood disorders and provide practical tools for overcoming anxiety and depression and renewing our minds.

MOOD DISORDERS

Anxiety disorders affect about 3 to 4 percent of the population and are twice as prevalent in women compared to men. Symptoms of anxiety include irritability, sleep disturbances, muscle tension, restlessness, fatigue, and difficulty with concentration. Anxiety is the body's response to a perceived threat, which results in a release of adrenaline from the amygdala, part of the fight-or-flight response, which helps you perform in dangerous or stressful situations. However, the brain is unable to differentiate between a *real* and an *imagined* threat. Thus, negative thought patterns (an inability to take your thoughts captive) can cause chronic releases of adrenaline and cortisol, which affect the neurotransmitter (brain chemicals) balance in the brain.

Depression is characterized by persistent or recurrent feelings of sadness or hopelessness, loss of ability to perceive pleasure, and reduced energy level; it is also often associated with low self-esteem. The average lifetime risk of developing depression is about 8 to 12 percent, and depression is twice as common in women as compared to men. Depression is a risk factor associated with certain physical conditions, and people who suffer from depression have shorter life expectancies than the general population. Further, people who suffer from depression have been found to have abnormal brain neurotransmitters, which are very important chemicals that allow one brain neuron to communicate with another.

BODY, MIND, AND SPIRIT

Although anxiety and depression are separate entities, many people suffer from both conditions. Chronic anxiety can lead to depression, and people who are depressed can become anxious. Although we may think of mood disorders as being a psychological or spiritual condition, the fact is that we are triune beings. We are body, mind, and spirit, and we "think" from all three of these areas. When I see a patient in my office with a mood disorder, one of the first things I try to do is determine the root cause of that person's mood disorder. I have found that anxiety and depression can be rooted in a physical cause, such as hormonal or endocrine dysfunction. On the other hand, a dysfunctional family background or abuse may be a psychological cause for someone struggling with recurrent depression. Lastly, chronic sin patterns open people up to demonic oppression, which also affects mood. These three areas are interconnected, and illness in one area, particularly if present for an extended period of time, will often affect the other areas as well.

The main point I am trying to make here is that the brain is a very complex physical organ that is susceptible to physical injury or disease like other organs in our body. Certain chemical or hormonal imbalances, physical conditions, and brain injuries can directly cause mood disorders. In such situations, correcting the underlying imbalance, if possible, or providing medication may be the treatment of choice. I find that Christians are often reluctant to take medications for anxiety or depression, which can be quite unfortunate. I've seen so many people get their lives back once they started a medication that balanced their neurotransmitters.

Can you imagine telling a woman in your congregation who was a diabetic that if she just spent more time with God, prayed a bit more, and believed certain Scriptures that she would not have to take insulin? We wouldn't do that because we understand that diabetes is a physical condition caused by a decreased ability of the pancreas to make insulin. This same analogy is true for some people with mood disorders. The brain is an organ that is subject to physical injury or chemical or hormonal imbalance that can cause anxiety or depression. In certain circumstances, medication can be very helpful in correcting underlying neurotransmitter imbalances, which allow the brain to function normally again.

In other situations, lifestyle modification, counseling, prayer, meditation, and renewing the mind with some of the tools listed below are better treatment choices. I do recommend that people see their medical provider for a thorough physical exam and laboratory work-up to eliminate potential physical causes of any underlying mood disorder that is persistent.

One additional point I'd like to make here is that fear is the sin of unbelief—probably the most socially acceptable sin in the Church. I think if we are honest, we all struggle with varying levels of unbelief in certain areas of our lives, some more than others. But anxiety is fear, and Jesus Himself told us not to worry. Paul also said, *"Do not be anxious about anything..."* (Phil. 4:6). The bottom line is that when we worry, what we are saying is that we don't believe our God is good or that He will come through for us.

WHAT'S IN A THOUGHT?

Did you know that every thought has a corresponding electro-chemical reaction in your brain? When you think, powerful chemicals course through your body, having either a positive or a negative effect. When you have a particular "feeling," you need to understand that the feeling is being generated by your thoughts. You can't always control your feelings, but you can control your thoughts. That is why Paul said,

> *We demolish arguments and every pretension that sets itself up against the knowledge of God, and we take captive every thought to make it obedient to Christ* (2 Corinthians 10:5).

I find it helpful to think of our feelings as fruit that grows from a tree. Joy and peace are the fruit that is produced from a tree of faith in the goodness of God. If we believe that, no matter our circumstances, God is faithful, then we have access to the fruit of joy and peace. However, if in our minds the tree of unbelief prospers, then we will harvest the fruit of fear, hopelessness, and other negative emotions.

Most people are not consciously aware of their thoughts. In other words, about 85 percent of what we are thinking about is in our subconscious, and this is what we need to take captive. If we are feeling anxious or depressed, there are underlying thought patterns that are generating those feelings or "fruit." As we consciously change what we are thinking about, it may feel awkward at first, and we may not feel anything positive for a couple of hours. This is because, when we are thinking negatively, we have started a cascade of adrenaline, cortisol, and other negative chemicals that can take a couple of hours to dissipate. In this case, we need to just hang with it. As we think in a positive manner, our positive thoughts will generate positive chemicals that will in turn generate other neurotransmitters that will make us feel good. It may just take a bit of time to stop one cascade and generate another.

Another point I want to make here is that we must believe something to be true in order to obtain emotional benefit from that truth. This may seem obvious, but I come across many Christians who've memorized entire passages of Scripture on the faithfulness of God, but are full of unbelief. I had a gentleman in my office who rattled off the entire Psalm 91 in tears as he described to me his anxiety and how distant he felt from God. We can't just know truth; we have to believe it to be true for us.

Lastly, we need to consciously examine our thoughts and test them. We need to ask ourselves, "What is the origin of the thought? Does the thought line up with what God says? What is the motivation behind the thought? Is it love?" First John 4:1-18 describes how we can come under the subtle influence of an evil spirit and how perfect love casts out fear. I find that the enemy often comes to us with true statements that are perverted with accusation. We accept these accusations against us as just and deserving, not realizing the source. Taken at face value, the thoughts seem true, but the spirit behind the thoughts is punishment. If we feel condemnation with our thoughts, it is not the Holy Spirit,

> *Therefore, there is now no condemnation for those who are in Christ Jesus, because through Christ Jesus the law of the Spirit of life set me free from the law of sin and death* (Romans 8:1-2).

The Holy Spirit brings correction, but He does so in a way that does not make us feel dirty, afraid, or punished. Those types of feelings come from the enemy. Thus, the origin of our thoughts is critically important—something we must be continually checking on and aware of. Our enemy is very deceptive, and usually he has some element of truth in his whispers. The devil even tempted Jesus in the desert with the very Scriptures themselves; he just used them out of context. Truth out of context is no longer truth.

In summary, many people suffer from both anxiety and depression, and these mood disorders can be rooted in our physical bodies, our minds, or our spirits. Every thought we have has a corresponding chemical reaction and our thoughts generate our feelings, which is why we need to take our thoughts captive. Also, it's not enough to know truth; we have to believe the truth to actually get emotional benefit from that truth. Lastly, not all of our thoughts are our own. The origin of our thoughts is important to analyze; when we identify feelings of fear or punishment in our thoughts, we can recognize that they may be generated by an evil source.

In the last part of this chapter, I will discuss some tips for overcoming anxiety and depression.[1]

FORGIVENESS

An unwillingness to forgive someone for a past or even an ongoing hurt will lead to bitterness. Bitterness is like a vigorous vine that will grow in your mind and choke out the tree of faith we discussed earlier. Bitterness produces the fruit of hate, rage, resentment, judgment, and other negative emotions that release toxic chemicals into our brains that disrupt access to the feelings of joy and peace. Bitterness is like a cancer to our thought lives, quickly taking over our thoughts and emotions. We open ourselves up to bitterness when we become offended, so it's important to be quick to forgive.

This is why the Word says not to let the sun go down on our anger (see Eph. 4:26). We are likewise instructed in the Lord's Prayer to forgive those who trespass against us (see Matt. 6:12). There is an element of timeliness to forgiveness. Forgiveness is the antiseptic that keeps bitterness from taking hold, and even more powerfully, it can become the antibiotic that kills bitterness if it begins to infect. However, bitterness can do a lot of damage if it is allowed to root for an extended period of time. People who live their lives in bitterness see the world through a very distorted lens and are miserable to be around.

Forgiveness is often difficult. Our offenses may very well be justified. However, we forgive others, not because they deserve it, but because Christ forgave us. We also do not deserve forgiveness. When I think of what Christ did for me on the cross, I quickly toss out my arguments for why I should hold my offense against my brother or sister. It becomes much easier when I look at it from this perspective.

Another point I want to make about forgiveness is that we may need to do it out of obedience, and we may need to do it repeatedly before we feel the truth sink into our minds and spirits. Remember what we said earlier about believing something to be true before we experience the emotional benefit of that truth. When I am angry because I am offended, I stop my offended thoughts and forgive the person. Then, if I need to, I repeat it as I strategically work against both my flesh and the enemy and begin to pray a blessing on the person who caused me harm. I have experienced this strategy to be fairly effective when I find myself forgiving someone over and over again for the same offense.

Lastly, we must remember that not all our thoughts are our own. The enemy will often bring up past offenses to discourage, distract, or derail us. Have you ever been doing some task, minding your own business, when a random past memory of some offense comes up, an offense you've already forgiven? Pretty soon you've relived the entire offense in your mind, you're angry at the person you forgave several years ago, and now you feel dirty and guilty for your thoughts. You've been slimed by the enemy. This is one of his favorite strategies, and he does it easily and quickly if you do not "take your thoughts captive."

An effective way to deal with this is first to stop and remember the origin of the thought. Quickly forgive the person again if you feel angry. Then—here's the kicker—thank the enemy for reminding you of this person and how grateful you are for the forgiveness of Christ in your life and how you can extend it to others. Then pray for the blessing and prosperity of those who've hurt you in the past. I have found that this technique silences the enemy quite rapidly, causing those annoying past offenses to stop wounding and hounding me.

REMEMBER

A simple, but very powerful and easy way to access faith, peace, and joy is to go back into past positive memories of times when God blessed us, healed us, delivered us, protected us, or answered our prayers. When we access those memories, those thoughts release those same positive chemicals, and our faith is renewed. So we must spend time journaling, recording, and reading aloud our victories in Christ. This is how we build up our faith. In fact, David did this repeatedly throughout the Psalms. Many of the Psalms start off with David being weary and downcast, questioning whether God even remembers him. Then David recounts a past point of victory and moves his soul to a place of worship and faith. He does this by simply remembering.

Where has God come through for you in the past? Where has He protected you? What prayers has He answered? Instead of focusing on what God has not done, focus on what He has done. That is where you will find your faith and joy. If you are having a hard time remembering what God has done for you, you can still benefit from this technique by remembering what He has done for others.

Express the Word

The power of life and death is in the tongue (see Prov. 18:21), and we do create worlds with our words. We absolutely need to guard our tongues so that what we speak lines up with what God's Word says. Our words have power, and we can either restrain or empower demonic forces with our words.

God's Word is living and active, so I encourage my patients to read aloud key Scriptures that speak to their situations. There is something powerful about reading the Word of God out loud. *"Faith comes by hearing, and hearing by the Word of God"* (Rom. 10:17 NKJV). When I see the Word, it enters my brain through one pathway, but when I read it out loud, it enters my brain through an additional pathway, and the truth is compounded.

If you are struggling with fear, find a Scripture that speaks to your fear—such as, *"I sought the Lord and he answered me; he delivered me from all my fears"* (Ps. 34:4)—and read it out loud over and over again until it rings true in your spirit. You may read it twenty times or more until you feel your mind come into agreement with your spirit.

We need to let our spirits lead our minds, because our spirits will often recognize truth before our minds can perceive it. Bill Johnson says our spirits make a better leader and our minds a better follower. In mood disorders, this leadership is often reversed. The spirit is trailing the mind. If you're struggling with this, tell your natural mind to take a rest and command your spirit to follow the Holy Spirit. Then read and express the Scriptures with this in mind. David often did this in the Psalms. He would command his "soul" or his mind to praise the Lord. You can almost see him grab himself by his lapels and tell his soul what it was going to do. Your spirit needs to lead your mind.

NOURISH YOUR MIND

Out of the heart, the mouth speaks (see Luke 6:45). Thus, we must consider what we are feeding our minds and hearts. In other words, what are we reading, watching, and listening to? Paul said,

> *Rejoice in the Lord always...do not be anxious about anything... and the peace of God which transcends all understanding will guard your hearts and minds in Christ Jesus* (Philippians 4:4-7).

Then Paul goes on to say how to do this—by nourishing our minds with thoughts of whatever is true, noble, pure, right, lovely, admirable, excellent and praiseworthy (see Phil. 4:8).

We must be very careful what we give our minds access to. We are surrounded 24/7 by media that focuses on the negative, because that's what sells. I'm not saying that we should not be aware of what's happening in the world around us, but we must check our spirits. If what we're listening to or watching is making us feel anxious, fearful, sad, angry, or powerless and does not meet the criteria listed by Paul above, then let's turn it off. Instead, let's surround ourselves with worship music, God's Word, uplifting or encouraging books, CDs, sermons, and so forth. In other words, we should build up our faith and guard our hearts and minds.

GRATITUDE

It is difficult to be grateful and to be anxious or depressed. I've found that people who are routinely thankful are generally happy and seem to be immune from anxiety and depression. When we are able to find what is right in the world around us and to be thankful for that, we've found a key to happiness. Our culture trains us to look at problems so we can fix them, but the reality is that we are surrounded by amazing blessings that we routinely overlook. We think nothing of flipping a switch to control the heating or air conditioning for our comfort, calling our friends or relatives on the telephone when we want to talk, or traveling by airplane or auto—all of which were unavailable one hundred years ago. We have much to be thankful for. The breakthroughs in medicine, science, and technology in the past one hundred years are unprecedented. The Kingdom of God is also expanding throughout the earth. Again, we have much to be thankful for. Thanksgiving resets our mind and helps us to focus on the positive. Thanksgiving also allows us to enter into God's presence, as Psalm 100 tells us: *"Enter his gates with thanksgiving and his courts with praise; give thanks to him and praise his name"* (Ps. 100:4).

The simple act of thanking God for our blessings positions us to enter into worship. I think of thanksgiving as the gateway to worship. When I don't "feel" like worshiping God, I start by thanking Him for my many blessings. Pretty soon, my spirit and soul are in accord, and worship becomes natural. Gratitude is simple. Start by thanking God for at least five things every day, and try to find different things to be grateful for. Really look at the world around you and delight yourself in the abundance of the Lord's blessings in your life.

IMMERSE YOURSELF IN THE PRESENCE OF GOD

We become like the One we behold. Since God is not anxious, worried, or depressed, but is, in fact, joyful and full of faith and hope, His presence is a refuge. We must let the Holy Spirit renew our spirits. As David said, *"I sought the Lord and he answered me, he delivered me from all my fears. Those who look to him are radiant"* (Ps. 34:4-5). Just one moment in God's presence can renew our minds if we are feeling anxious or depressed and far from His presence. We can start with gratitude, and from there, move into worship, continuing in worship until we feel God's presence. The reality is that God's presence is with us all of the time. In fact, He is closer than we know. He dwells in us, and we have access to Him at all times.

WHAT ARE YOU WEARING?

Paul tells us in Ephesians 6 that we are in a battle and that we need to wear armor to ward off evil forces and to stand our ground. Sometimes all we can do is just hold our ground. Unfortunately, I see many people running around naked and wounded. They do not understand that they are in a battle, and they do not wear armor.

These are the ones who have forgotten to put on their helmet of salvation. They do not understand that the cross cleansed them from all of their unrighteousness, and they are no longer sinners, but saints. They always feel unclean because their minds are not protected by the blood of Jesus. They do not know the truth very well, so their pants don't stay up. Truth is critical, as it keeps things together. They do not realize that their sin patterns expose their hearts to the enemy. If they would repent, they could again wear their breastplate of righteousness. But their guilt opens them up to a spirit of fear and oppression.

Are you wearing shoes that promote the gospel of peace? Now that you have your armor on, you need your shield and your weapon. Your shield is powerful, and it is faith in God. This is how you fight unbelief. Faith is the antithesis of unbelief, and this shield protects your heart and your mind from the fiery darts of the enemy. In addition, you can go on the offense with your sword of the Spirit, which is the Word of God.

> *Finally, be strong in the Lord and in his mighty power. Put on the full armor of God so that you can take your stand against the devil's schemes. For our struggle is not against flesh and blood, but against the rulers, against the authorities, against the powers of this dark world and against the spiritual forces of evil in the heavenly realms. Therefore put on the full armor of God, so that when the day of evil comes, you may be able to stand your ground, and after you have done everything, to stand. Stand firm then, with the belt of truth buckled around your waist, with the breastplate of righteousness in place, and with your feet fitted with the readiness that comes from the gospel of peace. In addition to all this, take up the shield of faith, with which you can extinguish all the flaming arrows of the evil one. Take the helmet of salvation and the sword of the Spirit, which is the word of God* (Ephesians 6:10-17).

CHRIST IN YOU

Do you really understand who Christ is in you? He actually lives in you. When I meditate on the book of Ephesians, my spirit soars, though my mind can scarcely grasp the glorious riches of my inheritance in Christ. What does it really mean to be blessed with every spiritual blessing in Christ? Or can you comprehend the power that raised Christ from the dead dwelling in you—or the fact that you are seated in heavenly places with Christ? I encourage you to spend some time meditating on the first three chapters of Ephesians, focusing on your inheritance and position as a believer in Christ. No matter your situation, nothing can separate you from the love of God.

Endnote

1. I would also like to recommend *Anxiety, Phobias and Panic: A Step-by-Step Program for Regaining Control of Your Life,* by Reneau Peurifoy. These tips are practical and are most helpful when done together. If they seem difficult or foreign to you, start with one and build on it, then add another, instead of trying to do them all at once.

Chapter 9

RAISING DISCERNING KIDS

Jenn Johnson

I HAVE THREE AMAZING CHILDREN—HALEY BREN (10), Téa Kate (7), and Braden Tyler (4)—and I love them so much! As their mom, my desire is to love them, teach them, and lead them into being amazing, world-changing people who are filled with love for others. I'm not just talking about when they're adults, but about right now. Our kids are powerful, and they have world-changing power within them. We need to help them realize their strengths and gifts, identify and work on their weaknesses, and recognize who they are in God—royal sons and daughters who belong to Him, reflect Him, and represent (re-present) Him to the world. As parents, our call is to encourage them ("to inspire with courage"[1]), to draw out the power within them, and to speak truth to them about who they are in God. If we do that as they grow up—if we teach them who they are as royalty and help them become aware of the King and Kingdom they represent—they will become influential people for Jesus. That's my goal with my kids—to set them on a path toward success in Kingdom living, even from a young age. After all, there's no age limit in the Holy Spirit.

NO AGE LIMIT

Our children's ministry at Bethel Church wrote an amazing declaration for the kids that calls out the powerful potential within them:

I am powerful, and what I believe changes the world!
So today I declare:

God is in a good mood.

He loves me all the time.

Nothing can separate me from His love.

Jesus' blood paid for everything.

I will tell nations of what He has done.

I am important.

How He made me is amazing.

I was designed for worship.

My mouth establishes praise to silence the enemy.

Everywhere I go becomes a perfect health zone.

And with God, nothing is impossible![2]

As this declaration, which is based on Scripture shows, our kids (and grandkids) have the same Holy Spirit living in them as we do. This is really important. And it's something we need to live out in our daily lives. But first we have to believe it. I'm not talking about simply agreeing with it in our minds, but about living like we believe it. I'm talking about taking kids seriously and not diminishing them because of their age. The apostle Paul wrote to his spiritual son, Timothy, *"Don't let anyone look down on you because you are young..."* (1 Tim. 4:12). We need to apply this to our relationships with children as well. We need to really believe what Jesus said: *"Truly I tell you, unless you change and become like little children, you will never enter the kingdom of heaven"* (Matt. 18:3).

I am thankful for my mother-in-(~~law~~)love, Beni, who taught me, when our kids were really little, that a great deal of the stuff kids feel is spiritual. It's so easy to become frustrated with our children when we don't understand why they're doing what they're doing. Their emotions are still immature, and they don't understand *why* they feel what they feel most of the time. To us, if we don't have eyes to see what's really going on, it can seem irrational, like hormones or tiredness. If we don't have a grid or a value for their ability to see and discern in the Spirit, we will "misdiagnose" them and shut them down. But if we want to raise children who are world-changers, we need to find a different response.

INTERCESSION 101:
TEARS FOR THE HOMELESS

Once, when Haley was around three years old, I was driving in the car with her and Beni. Suddenly Haley started sobbing in her car seat for seemingly no reason. I said, "What in the world?" And like most moms, I began thinking, *Oh, she must be tired. She didn't sleep well last night.*

But Beni said, "There's something to this." She turned around to face Haley in her car seat, and she asked, "When did you get sad? What made you sad?"

When Beni asked her that question, Haley suddenly became aware that her sadness may have been caused by something outside of her. I could see the realization in her eyes. In that moment, she had a spiritual awakening to the realm of discernment. Haley said, "That guy back there. He made me really sad."

Instantly both Beni and I realized that Haley had started crying right as we passed a homeless man on the street. We hadn't even noticed the connection until she mentioned him. Now we were on to something.

We could have just ignored her emotional response by saying, "Oh, it'll be okay, honey," or something like that. But we recognized the Spirit at work, and we engaged the opportunity. Our car ride had turned into Intercession 101. This was Beni's response to little Haley, our intercessor in training: "You've been able to feel that sadness so that you can know how to pray. But the sadness isn't yours. Now we need to place that sadness back in Jesus' hands because that's His to carry, not yours." Beni had Haley close her eyes, and then she continued, "Haley, I want you to take all the sadness you're feeling and put it back in Jesus' hands. Can you see it there?"

"Yeah," Haley said.

"Now you can pray," said Beni.

Beni had Haley extend her hand toward the homeless man, who was across the parking lot, and she led her in a simple prayer: "Jesus, we release peace to him."

"How do you feel now?" Beni asked.

"Good!" Haley said. The tears were gone; a smile had taken over. And Haley had learned an important lesson about her emotions and about the Spirit of God. As you will see in another story I tell later in this chapter, she has continued to grow in this, even as she has gotten older. My husband, Brian, and I have worked hard to practice this spiritual training with our kids in the day-to-day situations of life. It's a learning process—all of us learning to listen to the Holy Spirit.

Intercession 201: Sadness in the Fire Hall

More recently, when our second daughter, Téa, was six, I had a similar experience with her. I was a chaperon for a school field trip to the fire department, and I was driving several other kids, along with Téa. On the way, we were rocking out and dancing in the car, just having fun. We arrived, and they were all still goofing off. However, the minute we entered the firehouse, Téa went into her shell. She became sad, and she started pouting and being naughty. I thought, *Seriously?! What a field trip. You were just fine in the car, so what the heck?* We went through the tour and the presentation, and the whole time, Téa was acting out. Her teacher tried, to no avail, to get her to snap out of it. And I, of course, was frustrated. *Come on!* I thought. *Everyone's having fun. What's wrong with you?* At the end of the field trip, the teacher gave the kids donuts, but donuts didn't even cheer her up. I knew something was wrong.

After the donuts, we went back out to the car to leave, and as I was loading the kids into my car, I suddenly realized that "happy Téa" was back. Once again, she was bouncing and giggling with the other kids. The ride home was just like the ride there, with lots of fun and dancing in the back seat, and as I drove, I tried to figure out what had happened with her. I was struck by how she had suddenly become happy again in the car, and I felt the Lord whisper to me, "Pay attention to that." I realized something bigger was going on, and I knew I needed to take her home to talk about it.

I drove back to the school (because I still had the other kids with me). After returning the kids to their classroom, I pulled her aside and said, "Téa, school is going to be over soon anyway, so let's go home so mommy doesn't have to come back."

She said, "Alright," which is a miracle because usually she hates unexpected changes in the schedule. She likes to know what's happening, so no resistance from her was a sign and a wonder! (If you have a schedule-oriented child, you know what I mean!)

We went home, and I took her into her room, and I sat on the bed. I said, "You're not in trouble at all. I just want to talk to you about something. Tell me what was going on with you at the fire department."

Immediately, she went back in her shell, mumbling, "I didn't like it there."

"Why?" I asked.

"It was really sad in there," she said.

"Oh," I said, "You felt sadness in there." I looked her in the eyes. "Téa, you have an invitation to pray because God let you feel something that's not yours to keep." It was the same scenario as with Haley, but at an older age. I continued, "Téa, let's pray for those firefighters. This isn't your sadness. Put it in Jesus' hands." After she had prayed, I asked her, "How do you feel, Téa?"

"Good!" she said, skipping out of my arms and out of the room.

This experience with Téa looked different from Haley's experience on the outside. Téa didn't cry, but just went into her shell. There's no formula for how our kids will respond when they are sensing something spiritually. What is certain is that they will feel things that are bigger than them. They will pick up on other people's pain and the way God feels toward people. It's easy to say, "Oh, she's just tired," or "She's just having a bad attitude," but our kids' emotions are not always that simple. If we always interpret them on a surface level, we will miss a great deal, and our kids will be frustrated, too, because we aren't helping them understand why they're feeling what they're feeling.

DISCERNING THE SOURCE

The question that Beni asked Haley is the key. "When did you start feeling sad?" In other words, you need to show your kids how to go back and find their peace. Help them to figure out when and why they started feeling sad or angry—or whatever emotion they're manifesting that's outside of their character. Go back and find it. Then you will know how to deal with it. Stop what you're doing and ask the Holy Spirit what's going on—what spiritual reality is your child discerning? Once you identify the source, ask the Holy Spirit what you need to do or pray for.

Many of us have experienced times when we started "randomly" feeling a certain way, but we didn't know why. You walk into a store and suddenly start feeling discouraged for no reason, even though previously you were very hopeful. You go to a church service and begin having all sorts of judgmental thoughts about other people there, but normally you are a very grace-filled person. These are examples of what spiritual discernment can look like, and it's something that everyone experiences. That is why unbelievers are often drawn to Christians who carry a lot of peace and joy. They can sense it; they feel good when they are with these believers, but they don't fully understand why.

Kids are the same way, and often they are more discerning than adults because they have not yet learned to rationalize away what they feel. I'm not saying that every emotion our kids have is spiritual discernment. Obviously, anyone who has kids knows that is not true. So this is not a cut-and-dried formula, but something we need to be aware of so that we can hear the Holy Spirit's voice calling attention to our kids' emotions when they *are* springing from discernment. As I saw, in both of my experiences with Haley and Téa, the discernment was marked by uncharacteristic behavior and a sudden shift in emotion. If you are looking at your child and thinking, *What is going on? Why are you suddenly acting like this?* it's time to ask the Holy Spirit what's going on. Chances are, your child is acting out more than simple childhood disobedience.

When kids begin to understand discernment, they start to realize that they can hear from the Lord just as well as the adults. This empowers them to begin partnering with the Holy Spirit and to believe in their ability to change the world at any age. An experience that I had with Téa when she was six solidified the importance of this in my heart. At that time, Téa was working through her tendency to respond in anger when she became frustrated with other people. It had been a long process, and I had come to the end of my rope with training and disciplining her.

One Sunday I told her, "Téa, you need to ask the Holy Spirit to speak to you about this." During worship at church that same morning, Téa got a word from God, and she wrote it down on her bulletin: "Keep your patience." To me, *keep* implies *maintain*. In other words, "Maintain patience by going to God for things." When she showed it to me, I was amazed because God had spoken to her in a way that I never could have. He had touched her heart with His wisdom, and that made all the difference. I had given Téa everything I knew to give her, but what she needed was a word from God. As parents, we do our best to give our kids wisdom, love, and discipline, but we must remember that the same Holy Spirit who lives in us also lives in them and is speaking to them. I believe sometimes children can even hear more clearly than adults because of their simplicity.

It's our job to teach the kids in our lives what it looks like to listen to the Holy Spirit and how to recognize when they are feeling an emotion that isn't theirs. This takes lots of work, lots of consistency; it's a learning experience. But the reward is incredible! Kids who have learned to understand their discernment and to listen to the Holy Spirit are unstoppable. This ability, plus their childlike faith in the impossible, makes them powerhouses for Jesus who will truly impact people with God's love.

INTERCESSION 301: TREASURE HUNT IN TARGET

As I said previously, our oldest daughter, Haley, has continued to grow in her understanding of spiritual discernment. Often it manifests in small ways, but on one particular instance, I got to see the power of teaching our kids to understand and act on their discernment.

On Mother's Day 2011, my family was at church, sitting on the front row. The worship team was tuning up, and the service was about to start. My father-in-love, Bill, got up to greet everyone, and he said, "It's Mother's Day today! Bless the mothers around you!" Everyone began turning around to greet the mothers, clapping and hugging. In the midst of this, I turned to put my stuff down on my chair before worship, and I noticed that Haley was bawling. She was nine at the time, and she's not an overly emotional child (in a negative way), but is very balanced, so this was unusual for her.

Clearly something was wrong. I took her out to the hall and asked, "Hey, what's going on with you?"

She said, through her tears, "We need to go home right now!"

Worship was about to start, and this was not what I wanted to hear. It is hard work and most weeks a miracle to not only have three kids who are healthy, but to also get all of us to church and into the nursery on time. Miraculously, that had happened that day. I wanted to enjoy it.

I said, "Do you feel like this is the Lord, or do you feel like this is something that you're feeling personally as a need?"

"The Lord," she said firmly.

"Okay. Then I don't need to know all the answers," I said. As we walked out, I told her, "Baby, sometimes in following the Holy Spirit and following what He says, you don't have to have the A to Z of the plan. You just have the A, so let's honor that."

Honoring my kids is something I'm still learning—especially when I want to be at church on Sunday morning to be with and worship with our church body. That morning there were a lot of factors that were telling me not to leave, but I knew there was something to what Haley had said. I could feel it. So I decided to just go with it and trust her and the Holy Spirit speaking to her. I told Brian I was taking her home, and she and I left.

At that time, we lived really close to the church, and I spent the short drive home trying, in my head, to figure out what we were doing. It's so easy, when we hear something that doesn't make sense to our natural minds, to try to rationalize it. I thought to myself, *Last week somebody broke into my nanny's car in front of my house. We're going to go home and catch these people red-handed. Where's my crowbar?* I began mentally preparing to kick someone's butt, but of course, I didn't let Haley know the emotions and thoughts running through my head.

When we got home, everything was perfect—no vandals or thieves to catch red-handed. I was stumped. *Why are we here?* I wondered. I told Haley, "Here's what we're going to do. The Holy Spirit is letting you feel something. Let's see if we're supposed to just come home and that's it, or if He has something else for us to do today."

She said, "Okay."

I told her, "I want you to go sit on the couch and start speaking in tongues. Ask the Holy Spirit, 'Are we done, or do we have something else to do?'"

"Okay," she said, and she did.

While I waited on her, I put some clothing in the dryer because it needed to be done. (All the moms know what I'm talking about!) This wasn't my deal, but Haley's, and she needed to get her answer for herself. After a while, I went back in and said, "All right. What are you feeling?"

She said, "I feel like I'm supposed to ask you what the first business is that you think of. The first store."

Honestly, I was starting to feel a little impatient, but was trying to be supportive. It just did not make any sense to me, but I closed my eyes and said the first store that came to mind—Target. What she said next gave me the chills.

She sat up on the couch and said, "We're going to Target, and we're going to find a lady with brown hair who has a deep sadness in her heart and needs to know that Jesus is meeting her there, and her name starts with an M or an N."

I was floored. "Whoa! Okay! Let's go!" We jumped in the car and drove the few minutes to Target, pulled in the parking lot, got out, and went into the store. We were ready for our Holy Spirit adventure! I said, "All right, here's what we're going to do. We're just going to shop, and if we see someone you think could be her, we'll just go up to her and tell her we're on a treasure hunt and we're looking for someone with an M or N name. It may take trying a few people, so don't get discouraged if we don't find her instantly."

She was cool with that, so we got our cart and began walking. It wasn't long until we encountered our first lady. I said, "Hi, we're on a treasure hunt, and we're just looking for someone with a name that begins with M or N."

She said, "No, I'm sorry. It's not me. Have fun."

So we kept going. We asked a second lady, who said, "It's not me, but I totally know what you're doing. I go to Bethel."[3] She winked at us, and we grinned back.

"Let's keep trying," I said.

We turned the corner and saw a beautiful woman with dark brown hair who was really well-dressed walking toward us. I didn't tell Haley, because this was her deal and she needed to discern it on her own, but in my spirit, I felt certain she was the one. *Oh yeah, we have a winner,* I thought.

As we approached this woman, I felt great sadness over her. I knew for sure she was our reason for being in Target on Mother's Day morning, but I still didn't tell Haley.

Haley looked at me and said, "I think this is the one."

I nodded back. "Let's do this!" I said. So we cornered this woman in the towels.

I said, "Hi, my daughter and I are here on a treasure hunt. We're looking for someone with a name starting with M or N."

I could tell she had no idea it was a spiritual treasure hunt. It wasn't on her grid at all. She said, "Oh! My name is Nancy."[4]

Haley looked at me, looking for a cue, and I encouraged her, saying, "Haley, why don't you tell this woman what you were feeling today and what you were seeing."

So Haley said, "I was in church today, and my Papa [Grandpa] started talking about mothers, and I just got really sad." Haley continued, "I went home and asked God what this was about. I saw a woman with brown hair who had a deep sadness in her heart that she didn't want to talk about. I knew that the Lord knew where she was at and was meeting her in that sadness. And I knew that her name started with an M or an N."

Nancy clearly had no box for what was happening, but I could tell that Haley's words were like a shot to her heart. Her eyes filled with tears. She was speechless. God had touched this woman through an unassuming nine year old. Kids can often speak to people in places and situations for which adults have no grace. I asked, "Do you mind if she prays for you?"

"Sure! That'd be great," Nancy said, still shocked.

Haley then put her hand on Nancy and released the fire of God in a nine-year-old package. It was awesome. She prayed, "Lord, I pray that You would meet her with happiness where she's feeling sad…." She prayed a whole prayer full of exactly what Nancy needed to hear. On the inside, I was shouting, *YES!* I didn't say a word. I didn't need to. Haley had prayed over her perfectly. I knew that her words were accurate, that the Holy Spirit was using her powerfully to speak His love to this broken woman. I didn't need to add anything.

When Haley was done, Nancy simply said, "You came here for me." She was at a loss for words. She said, again, "You came here just for me. Thank you so much." Smiling, Haley and I told Nancy we loved her, and we blessed her. Then we left the store shouting, "YEAH! WAHOO!" What a Holy Spirit adventure!

Once we were done rejoicing, I said, "Haley, you know what the best Mother's Day present in the whole wide world is?"

She said, "What?"

I said, "You listening to the Holy Spirit."

We all have an invitation to listen and follow His voice—not just the adults, but the kids, too.

Endnotes

1. *Merriam-Webster Dictionary Online,* s.v. "encourage"; http://www.merriam-webster.com/dictionary/encourage (accessed May 15, 2012).

2. "Offerings of Thanks #4," *Bethel Redding;* http://bethel-redding.com/offering-readings (accessed April 25, 2012).

3. To learn more about the Treasure Hunts that happen at Bethel, check out Kevin Dedmon's book, *The Ultimate Treasure Hunt* (Shippensburg, PA: Destiny Image, 2007).

4. Her name has been changed to protect her identity.

Chapter 10

WALKING IN GOD'S FAVOR

Dawna DeSilva

I HAVE BEEN IN AN AMAZING season of ministry favor for some time now. Much of which, I'm sure, has less to do with my awesomeness (though I wouldn't mind taking all the credit) and more to do with the fact that I am simply associated with Bethel Church here in Redding. Because favor often comes in these seasons when God is visibly moving, it can be easy to become impressed with ourselves. When I travel, people sometimes recognize me, stop me, hug me, and say, "Oh, my gosh—I've seen you on your videos. I've heard you speak. I know you. You are awesome!"

Actually, it can be funny at times. I was on a plane one day, and I went into the lavatory. I stayed in there a little while longer than the normal plane etiquette because my stomach had been hurting. Finally, I thought, *OK, I'd better get out of here.*

As I stepped out, somebody said my name, "Dawna. Dawna DeSilva." It was the flight attendant.

I thought, Yeah, I was in there so long she probably went and checked the passenger list.

But the flight attendant went on to say, "I've seen you. I know you! You're the Sozo Lady!"[1]

"Yes," I laughed. "I'm the Sozo Lady. Good to see you."

Another time, after I had given a talk in a city, a gentleman came up to me. He clasped my hands in his and began, "Oh, you changed my life! You're so amazing. I just poured out my heart to you, and God showed up."

The whole time this man was relating his freedom story, I was trying to remember who he was. Although I do meet thousands of people, I was expecting my brain to kick in at any moment and rescue me from my awkward silence. Instead, I just kept drawing a blank. It must have showed on my face because finally he dejectedly said, "You don't remember me, do you?"

I had a quick decision to make: lie or truth. Knowing that lies do not usually work out, I opted for truth, "I am so sorry, but I do not remember you."

Then his wife hit him on the shoulder and said, "She's never met you, silly. It was from her tapes." He had listened to so many of our Sozo DVDs and teachings that he felt as though he knew me. He even believed I had ministered to him because, as he had poured out his heart in response to my recorded words, God had healed him and set him free. God had used me—without my knowing it—to help deliver this man!

That's what visible favor can look like.

But what if you believe you are walking in your life calling, and it seems like you could change the world—but nothing changes? What if you get a vision, a group of trusted people confirms it— "Yes, God wants you to go and write that book!"—and you write the book, but no one buys it? What if somebody gives you a prophetic word and you run with it, but no one pays any attention to what you do? Even a little opposition would be better than that, wouldn't it?

I am not talking about sitting around doing nothing and hoping that favor will land on you without any personal effort. I'm not talking about a person who gets a prophetic word about becoming the next president of the United States and then spends the next four years floating on an inner tube on Shasta Lake. No presidential talent scout is going to find that person on Shasta Lake, even if a scout should happen to come to Redding to visit us here at Bethel. A person who receives such a prophetic word would need to go to college and then get involved in government and gain experience. That person would have to *do* something with the vision to see it fulfilled. This is called stewarding a vision or prophetic word.

Instead, I am talking about someone who gets that same word, and it burns in her spirit like nothing has ever burned before. *This has to be right. I know that's what I am supposed to do.* Off she goes to college, where she joins political organizations. Then she proceeds to lose every single political race she ever enters. For years! She can't even get elected to the local school board. What's up with that? Was it a false word? Did somebody miss a step? If a person is walking with God, this should easily work, shouldn't it?

When nothing seems to be happening, we ask all kinds of questions: How can we judge whether or not we are walking in our Heaven-sent destiny? What constitutes fulfillment of a word or of a call? How can we guard ourselves against the pitfalls of failure, even perceived failure? As we look at what we have to show for all of our effort and compare ourselves to others, how can we avoid falling into envy or shame? Or, once visible success breaks through, how can we avoid slipping into selfish ambition?

TWO EXTREMES

C.S. Lewis wrote that "The enemy always sends distractions in pairs...and that he relies on our extreme dislike for the one to propel us towards the other."[2] When we are pursuing our dreams, our call, and our destiny, and we are being blocked at every turn, it is so easy to get discouraged, hopeless, and bitter toward those who seem to "hog" all of God's favor.

The other extreme comes just as we are breaking through and walking out our dreams with our final destination in full sight. That's when the enemy tries to swing us toward selfish ambition, arrogance, and pride. What I have come to believe is that both extremes of these pairing distractions seem to play upon the same strings in our hearts—some variation on the theme of human favor.

When we feel like we have missed it or missed out, much of our dismay comes from the fact that we seem to have missed out on the praises and rewards of human approval. We feel worthless because nobody seems to have recognized the value of our efforts. We are distracted from hearing what God has to say about us because the voices inside our heads, which derives value from the reward system of the world, clamors so insistently in our brains. *They didn't notice you. You weren't good enough to be chosen. You will have to try harder. See—only they have God's favor....*

Alternatively, when we feel that we are riding the crest of a wave of success and that God's favor has lined up with the favor of the people around us, our distractions still come from an inner tendency to lean a little too much on what other people think or proclaim about us. *These people think I'm amazing? Then I must be. Wait, I don't want to act proud. Now where did my peace go? What are the other people thinking about me? Am I living up to everybody's expectations?*

We are so easily caught up in this inner conflict of trying to live between these two extremes. But it is hard for us to content ourselves with the circumstances in which we find ourselves if we are unable to take our focus away from human praise and put it on God's truths about each of us. Paul addressed this when he wrote to the believers in Philippi:

> *I have learned how to be content (satisfied to the point where I am not disturbed or disquieted) in whatever state I am. I know how to be abased and live humbly in straitened circumstances, and I know also how to enjoy plenty and live in abundance. I have learned in any and all circumstances the secret of facing every situation, whether well-fed or going hungry, having a sufficiency and enough to spare or going without and being in want* (Philippians 4:11-12 AMP).

Clearly, Paul did not take his cues from his circumstances. Sometimes, people were convinced he was like a god, and they tried to worship him. At other times, he suffered great physical injury. (Read Acts 14, where both extremes happen in the same chapter.) Like Paul, each one of us needs to learn the value of living in the in-between.

We must recognize that living in a culture like ours can feed our problem. In today's world, everything is evaluated: thumbs up; thumbs down. We seem to be absolute nobodies if we're not amazing at something. If we are not great, we are not good enough. The trouble is that kind of favor is entirely human, and the enemy loves to exploit it. He whispers to us when we are up as well as when we're down. He is the one who drives us toward self-pity, victimization, arrogance, vindication, and all the rest. And we seem to buy into these "distractions" very readily.

One day, I was driving in my car, and I was whining to the Lord, "God, how come everything comes with struggles? Am I not working hard enough? Is my performance sub-standard? Have I been hidden from your view and from your favor?"

And the Lord spoke clearly to my heart. He said, "Man's favor is not an indication of my love for you. Likewise, man's disfavor is not an indication that I'm not backing the plan for your life."

I almost stopped the car. What a revelation!

SEEING GOD FOR WHO HE IS

Let's say I have written a book, and it is not selling very well. I thought I wrote it at God's direction, with excellence. Other books by previously unknown authors are doing great; the authors are selling tons of them. I look at *The Shack;* that was a best seller, and nobody had heard of the author before he published it. I look at the Harry Potter series; what a phenomenal success, and it's not even life-giving. Then here is my book, which *is* life-giving and life-changing, and nobody will buy it. I am just giving it away. *God, I thought that writing that book was Your call on my life....*

God reminds me, "Man's shut doors do not indicate that this is not the call on your life."

If we don't get this, we had better watch out. Selfish ambition will come in and taunt us to start conceiving of new strategies to sell more books. It says things like: "Let me show you how to be important. You aren't knocking on enough doors. No one is going to go to bat for you. You are being held back. You need to find a way to prove that you are worth backing." If we listen to these voices, we will go from a place of partnering with a poverty spirit or an orphan spirit ("I have nothing, and nobody cares") to partnering with pride and self-sufficiency ("I am going to power through this; I'm going to prove to everyone who didn't back me that I am a winner"). Both of these extremes are sins because neither one sees God for who He is, and both extremes look at our circumstances through a human lens.

When I see God for who He is, I remember that I am small, and yet I find such a sense of value in His love for me. He is a God who loves you unconditionally, and He has loved you and entrusted you with being exactly (and only) the person He created you to be. You are not supposed to emulate anybody else. Knowing this when you hit the snags and distractions, you will be able to let them drive you back to Him instead of to the opposite paired forces. Ask Him, "What are *You* saying about this?" Then listen until you hear what He is saying about you and to you. His perspective is the only one that brings life.

We read in the Gospel of Luke that Jesus grew in favor with both God and man (see Luke 2:52). For years, I have prayed, "God, would you grow me in favor with both You and man?" I have a measure of favor with people; a flight attendant recognizes me, a man recognizes me from my DVDs, and some people have asked if they can actually touch me. Yet, reveling in the favor of people puts me in just as dangerous a place as feeling abandoned does. The enemy takes advantage of my concern with human favor either way. I need to learn how to walk humbly in the midst of people's favor and keep myself focused on God's favor, pressing past all the distractions that present themselves.

THE FATHER HAS NO ORPHANS

One of our biggest problems is thinking that our circumstances are bigger than our God is. When we think that way, we tend to wonder if our situation caught God unaware. We really need to take such thoughts captive and identify the orphan spirit that is behind them.

By *orphan spirit* I do not necessarily mean a literal demon named *orphan*. Instead, I am referring to *spirit* in terms of a prevailing worldview or a ruler or a power of the air spoken of in Ephesians 6. In the same way that you fight against demons, you combat these kinds of spirits by calling them by a name: *orphan spirit, poverty spirit, spirit of fear,* or whatever. You can identify the appropriate name for a spirit by evaluating what kind of perception saturates your thinking, influences your actions, and leads to the erroneous assumptions that underlay and typify your outlook on your circumstances. You will not find the terms *orphan spirit* or *spirit of poverty* anywhere in Scripture, but you can certainly find evidence of the mindset of poverty or the fingerprints of an orphan spirit. Think of *spirit* as the noun and *orphan* as the adjective. If you are affected by an orphan spirit, *orphan* is the attribute or quality that reflects itself in your life.

An orphan spirit causes a person to feel un-fathered or un-parented. Whole countries can live under a type of an orphan spirit. It makes people feel abandoned and unprotected so that they urgently try to protect themselves. After all, nobody else is going to do it because, according to the lens of an orphan spirit, all the nearby people are either orphans too, or they belong to a family that "the orphans" will never fit into.

To defeat an orphan spirit, you can't just turn your back on it and deny that it exists; you need to call it out. You must expose the lie that your Father in Heaven has forsaken you. Then you declare the truth that He will always look after you, unfailingly. Even when your circumstances remain the same, you cling to the validity of His watchful care and powerful provision. You nestle into His arms of love. How much better it is to move into an awareness of your Father God's favor than it is to worry so much about the favor of the people around you.

CLOUD OF WITNESSES

Walking in God's favor will automatically mean that you also enjoy the favor of some people, because you will be walking in the favor of those who have learned to walk in His favor. Even if you cannot recognize such people around you, they are always there, unseen:

> *Since we are surrounded by so great a cloud of witnesses, let us lay aside every weight, and the sin which so easily ensnares us, and let us run with endurance the race that is set before us, looking unto Jesus, the author and finisher of our faith, who for the joy that was set before Him endured the cross, despising the shame, and has sat down at the right hand of the throne of God* (Hebrews 12:1-2 NKJV).

They are cheering you on as you run the race that He has set before you. The One who endured the pain and humiliation of the crucifixion is standing there, too. When you stumble or fall, He picks you back up. It's a love relationship through and through, and that's the only kind of favor you will need.

I think about the cloud of witnesses when I'm struggling. When I'm grappling with problems and fears and I wonder if God is still approving of me, I can remember the faithfulness of those who have gone before me, and I can almost hear them cheering me on: "Go! Go! Go!" Their approval lets me know that everything is going to be okay and that, if I keep the eyes of my spirit on God Himself, my race will end well.

Once, I was chatting with someone, and he said, "You know, when I get to Heaven, I'm going to ask God all of my questions. Then I'll find out why He did certain things down here on earth." Suddenly, I got really quiet. "What's up?" he asked.

I answered, "I'm more worried about the questions He has for me when I get there." I was not saying that from a fear of failure, but more from the perspective of possible regret. Will I get there and find out what I could have been, where I could have gone, what I could have done for Him and with Him?

I suppose that there's not one person in the world—except Jesus Himself—who can fulfill every aspect of his or her destiny. Perfection is not the goal. But dreaming with Him is—*with Him.* It's a love relationship that will never end. What if we let the living of that love relationship become our principal destiny? That would put everything else into perspective, and the paired distractions would have no hold on us. What if we truly set aside rejection, shame, fear, performance, perfectionism, bitterness, and jealousy? What if we walked in a manner worthy of our Lord, both when we experienced favor and when we felt like favor was being withheld?

What if…

> *What if God, although choosing to show his wrath and make his power known, bore with great patience the objects of his wrath—prepared for destruction? What if he did this to make the riches of his glory known to the objects of his mercy, whom he prepared in advance for glory—even us, whom he also called?* (Romans 9:22-24)

What if…

What if every one of us lived the rest of our lives believing that we are clothed in His righteousness, forgiven, redeemed in every way, and so thoroughly loved by our Father in Heaven that it wouldn't matter what other people think of us? We might actually change the world.

Endnotes

1. Sozo is the inner healing and deliverance ministry of Bethel Church, and I'm the founder and co-leader of

this now international prayer ministry. The Greek word *sozo* means "saved, healed, delivered."

2. C.S. Lewis, *The Complete C.S. Lewis Signature Classics* (New York: HarperCollins, 2002), 150.

DESTINY PRAYERS

Jesus, thank You for Your presence surrounding me. I know that Your heart is to set people free, so I ask that Your Spirit would lead me as I pray. Without Your anointing, the words will be empty, but with Your anointing, they carry Your power and freedom. Make my heartbeat match yours. I love You, Lord. Amen.

Spirit of God, I want to soak in Your presence so that my spirit can be enlarged. I want to be able to hold more of You. I speak to my own spirit, and I say, "Wake up!" Fill my spirit with Your Spirit so much that all of the junk inside me gets squeezed out. I want to be able to hear Your voice better, and I want it to make a difference in my life.

In the name of Jesus, I break off the other voices (fear, condemnation, guilt, worthlessness, and others) that take my attention away from Your voice. You make all things new, and I am forever grateful to You. Amen.

*L*ord, I invite You to remind me throughout the day to protect my thoughts and to take them captive to You. Spirit of Truth, give me spiritual eyes to see the strategies of the enemy. Show me what is happening so that I don't get sucked into old lines of thinking. Show me how to use all of my spiritual armor and all of the tools you have taught me how to use, including forgiveness.

Lord, I chose to forgive the person who is coming to mind right now. I feel the injustice of the past situation, and I tend to hold onto it. That person doesn't even know he/she hurt me. It isn't easy to say "I forgive," but I want to say it. Forgive me for holding things against him/her. I repent of doing that. I release this person to your loving care. I bless him/her with every blessing—blessing in relationships, in finances, in health, in spiritual strength. Draw this person closer to You. Thank You for Your forgiveness and for Your love. Thank You, Lord Jesus. Amen.

*K*eep me from taking my eyes off of Your cross. It is redemption to me and to anyone who calls on Your name, Jesus. Keep me from reverting in any way to the person I used to be. Keep me up to date on forgiving people. Even when they didn't do anything wrong, but I perceive that they wronged me, keep me from talking myself out of saying words of forgiveness. I choose to forgive, and I ask You to redeem my relationships.

I know that this is a key to freedom. I know the feeling of being locked in prison with unforgiveness, and I know the sound of the click of the key when the door of my cell begins to open—the moment I say "I forgive him" or "I forgive her" or "I forgive them."

Remove from me any guilt-producing condemnation that has stained my spirit. Pour your soothing peace over my tormented mind and heart. Forgive me for trying on my own strength to wrestle down the very things that You wanted to erase from my internal sin inventory. I break off the performance thinking that makes me try to earn Your love and approval. I ask You to fill me up with the very things that the enemy tried to steal.

I declare faith, hope, and love into my own spirit. I declare courage into my spirit as well, along with the ability to receive the goodness of God. How wonderful You are! I love You forever. Amen.

Father, with Paul's prayers for the Ephesians as my guide, I'm going to list the truths that apply to me because of who I am as Your child:

- *I am forgiven.*

- *I am holy.*

- *I am righteous.*

- *I am loved beyond comprehension. (When You see me, You see Your son, Jesus.)*

- *I am made in Your image, and I am the apple of Your eye. I am lovely.*

- *I am important. I am incomparable.*

- *I have access to Christ. (I am seated in heavenly places with Him, who has all things under His feet, and He sits at Your right hand, making intercession for me.)*

- *I have Your Spirit of wisdom and revelation, so that I might know You better.*

- *I am rich in the abundance of Your glory and grace.*

- *I am protected, shielded, and covered.*

- *I am Your Son's bride, and He pursues me with love.*

- *I am sealed by Your Holy Spirit for all eternity.*

This is my identity. This is who I am. This is what I move out of. This is where I take my position of faith. In You, amen.

Father God, You are my true Father. I ask You to make it possible for me to move into a greater awareness of Your love for me. I want to live my life in the light of Your affirming love.

You have shown me some of the ways that the people around me, including my own family, have labeled me and instilled a distorted belief system into my spirit. So many of my beliefs are flawed, and I am only beginning to realize what they are. I ask You to help me differentiate between Your truth and all of these other influences. Help me know what to do with them. Make it possible for me to abandon the lies and to replace them with Your living truth.

I speak to the core lies that have found a home in my spirit, soul, and body. I say "No" to anything that causes me to take the eyes of my heart away from Jesus. With every fiber of my being, I want to acknowledge Your lordship and to worship You for Your care and watchfulness over not only me, but also over all of Your children.

I can never repay You for all You have done; I can only follow You more closely every day of my life, as You show me how to come after You. Jesus is my Lord. Amen.

Jesus, I have believed a lie. I have believed that the favor of other people is the proof of God's love and I now repent of believing that. I hand over to You my envy, jealously, selfish ambition, competition, performance, perfectionism, and every other —ism, and I ask You, Holy Spirit, to teach me what God's favor looks like.

Father God, today I hand You all remnants of an orphan spirit. I hand You every thought that defies the truth that I am loved by You, that I am accepted through Christ by You, and that I have Your stamp of approval on my life. I say to the self-pity, "Stop it." I say to the victim spirit, "Stop it." Father God, touch me with Your love.

I ask right now that by Your Spirit You would come into the place where I learned my understanding about You and my thoughts of how You think of me. I pray that You would come into my mindset and into the core values from which I respond and that You would break off ungodly beliefs like breaking branches off a tree and that You would replace the whole tree of unbelief with a faith tree inside me.

I want to be free from rejection; free of fear; free of envy, jealousy, and selfish ambition. I want to be able to think in a new way, Your way. I want to grow in the knowledge that I am truly loved by my Father, and I pray that the orphan spirit will no longer get a hearing in my heart. I want to be so in love with Jesus that I will actually become like the prophetic words that I am speaking. Oh, yes! In Jesus' name, amen.

Father, I pray to You through Your Son and by the power of Your Spirit. I pray for Your Kingdom to transform everything around me and for Heaven to come on earth.

I declare heavenly revelation for inventions, strategies, and ideas that answer questions that the world around me is asking. I ask You to develop leaders who encourage new ideas and holy creativity. I declare that the believers around me will be free to explore new aspects of Your Kingdom, partnering with the Holy Spirit.

I repent for harboring a poverty mindset, independent thinking, and hopelessness. I turn toward You for the courage to take risks and the discernment to recognize opportunities that You have placed in my path. As I join my spirit to Yours, I know that You will shower favor, blessings, and increase upon me so that I can do my part to bring Heaven to earth and promote the Gospel of Jesus Christ.

I have full access to the King. Full access! And the King has full access to me.

Search me, God, and know me. Search me, know me, and lead me. I know that greater access comes with deeper knowledge. I can come farther into Your heavenly Kingdom when I know You. You can enter more deeply into me when I have opened myself to You.

So search me more thoroughly, mighty God. Come into my spirit and mind and dwell with me. Lead me according to Your everlasting way.

Holy Spirit, I welcome You to be in me as an overcoming Spirit, a hope-bringing Spirit, a vision-inspiring Spirit. Strengthen me inside the core so that I can move out with new courage and resolve. Help me to have a long view, seeing beyond my circumstances and seeing past people's behavior—perceiving with eyes of faith.

I pray not only for an awareness of Your favor, but for tangible favor with other people. I pray for good relationships with others, especially with the members of my own family. Enhance my relationships and instruct me so that I can bring righteous love and godly wisdom into every bond with another person.

Even as You have showed me my own destiny and helped me to step into it, I pray that You will show others what You want for their lives. I call out the names of my loved ones, near and far, and I request for them heavenly encounters. May angels abound around all of these prayed-for ones! May some of them become clear voices to their generation, countering the worldly messages of entitlement and self-sufficiency.

In Jesus' wonderful name, amen.

Father God, what has kept me frozen and unable to pursue the dreams You have given me? Would You give me a season of breakthrough and help me to identify and push past the blockages inside?

Stir up in my heart and mind whatever You may want to speak to me today, and help me hear Your voice. I lay down my disappointments, my unanswered questions, and my unresolved pain over broken relationships. I invite You to come into my heart and mind. Restore me and empower me to seek out Your vision for my life; give me specific plans for making it a reality.

More than anything, I want to have the freedom to pursue Your love. I believe that You want that for me, too. And I'm grateful for Your Holy Spirit's help and hope. I bless Your holy name, amen.

*H*oly Spirit, I love You. Thank You, Lord, that You break every chain. Thank You, God, that I have full access to You, that You hold nothing back from me, that You pursue me with such passion.

I ask that Your presence would meet me today, that I would just encounter You even now. I ask that You would give me a beautiful place, like a garden, where I can go to meet with You. I am looking for a place where I can spend time with You, talk with You, feel Your tenderness, and receive Your gifts.

I need a place where I can receive Your comfort, and also Your perspective on difficult situations in my life. I want to be able to lay down my burdens at Your feet, and I'm thinking of those particular situations that burden me the most. I cannot change them. Whether You change them or not, I want You to have them. I cannot carry the weight of them any longer. I entrust them to You. Do with them as you see fit. Those burdens are not my responsibility.

I also ask you to alert me when I start to carry the weight again. I realize that I might do that. I believe what the Word says, that You do not forsake the righteous, that You will not leave me begging for what I need.

Impart Your joy to me, Lord. I need more of that joy that comes from the secret place with You. I know it is part of my inheritance as Your child, but I need You to hand it to me; I don't know where to find it by myself. As I meet You in our special place, please increase the revelation of Your love to me. I truly want to know the width, length, height, and depth of Your endless love. With joy in my spirit, amen.

God and Creator, thank You for creating me and for instilling in me Your creative spirit. Thank You also for giving me a measure of Your understanding and insight so that I can speak for You in many different ways.

I pray that You will show me how you see me. Show me the gifts You have given me, and help me to appreciate them. Help me also to appreciate the gifts You have given to others in Your Body. May we all function together under Your direction, complementing and enhancing each other's expression of Your wonderful nature, honoring each other even as we honor You.

I pray that You will allow me to continue to share Your Kingdom for the rest of my life on earth. I want to be faithful to exercise the gifts You have given me with grace and generosity. I bless Your work inside me, through me, and around me. I extend my spirit to bless all the things that You are doing, even the things I do not understand. In Jesus and through Him, amen.

What else can I be thankful for, Lord? What do I have to offer? Make my spirit sensitive to Yours.

As You show me what You have placed in my hand, I am going to steward it. I am not going to go bury it to hide it away. Here it is. Show me where to plant it. Show me how to bury it so that it will grow. Hover over it, grow it, multiply the expression of Your love through it.

Let Your love rain down on it as it rains down on me, so that Your love will transform everything, even the things that nobody sees except You. May nothing that Your love touches die; may everything spring up with new life, becoming stronger and healthier and more secure.

I say, "Thrive!" to the plantings you have assigned me to watch over. I say, "Grace!" even to the plantings that have not sprouted yet. I speak life where nothing has ever grown before. Thank You for allowing me to co-labor with You. In the strength of the Prince of Peace, amen.

I love You, Lord, and I give You my heart. I believe what You say about me and I know that You speak truth. You are love. You are my all-in-all. I give You my affections, today and every day. I look to You for every provision and all protection.

I know that I am fearfully and wonderfully made, and I thank You, heavenly Father, for making me in Your image. All of Your works are marvelous and very good. I thank You that You have set a table before me, providing just the right nourishment for each season of my life, and that You anoint my head on a daily basis. My cup overflows with Your goodness.

I say yes and amen to Your promises and to everything that You paid for on the cross. I affirm that with You all things are possible. I say yes and amen to Your decision to create me to be just who I am and for summoning me to walk in Your grace. Thank You for giving me a destiny and a testimony. Thank You for blessing me and keeping me, for allowing Your face to shine upon me, for being so gracious to me. I am glad that You have lifted up Your countenance upon me and that You have given me true peace.

Surely goodness and mercy will follow me all the days of my life. I choose to follow You. I choose to steward my heart every day. With my whole heart (the heart You are making whole), I love You. I am so glad to be a child after Your own heart. Amen.

ABOUT BENI JOHNSON

Brenda (Beni) Johnson and her husband, Bill, are the Senior Pastors of Bethel Church. Together they serve a growing number of churches that have partnered for revival. This apostolic network has crossed denominational lines in building relationships that enable church leaders to walk in both purity and power.

Beni has a call to intercession that is an integral part of the Bethel Church mission. She is in charge of Bethel's Prayer House, ministry teams, and intercessors. The Lord has given her a heart for broken people of all ages. Her insight into strategies for prayer and her involvement in prayer networks have helped to bring much-needed breakthrough in Bethel's ministry.

Beni's heart is to help people begin to carry joy in intercession. She believes that being an intercessor is capturing the heartbeat of Heaven and declaring or praying that into your world. It is true agreement with Heaven. Beni has authored several books, including The Happy Intercessor and Beautiful One. Visit Beni's ministry website at www.benij.org, where you will find access to many resources and can view her travel itinerary. Beni and Bill have three adult children, who are all married and involved in ministry, and nine grandchildren.

About Sheri Silk

Sheri Silk is the new General Manager of Advance Redding, INC, a management company. This new public benefit non-profit is working alongside the city of Redding to manage the Redding Civic Auditorium. She also serves on the senior management team of Bethel Church, overseeing the Nursery and the Children's Department. She and her husband, Danny, are the founders of Loving On Purpose Educational Services, a ministry to families and communities worldwide. Visit Sheri and Danny's website, www. lovingonpurpose.com, for more information on their resources and travel schedule. They have been married for twenty-seven years and have three adult children and three grandchildren.

ABOUT THERESA DEDMON

Theresa Dedmon has a traveling ministry, both in the United States and abroad, which focuses on equipping and activating churches in how to step into their supernatural destiny. She activates churches in how to touch their community through creative expressions and love. She empowers people to go after their dreams and teaches them how God's supernatural creative power can be released in every part of church life, as well as in worship. She has her BA in Psychology, with a minor in Biblical Studies from Vanguard University, and she has been in pastoral ministry with her husband, Kevin, for over twenty-five years. She is currently on staff at Bethel Church in Redding, California, where she heads up all of the Creative Arts there and in Bethel's School of Supernatural Ministry. She is a sought-after conference speaker who releases people to be set free to walk in supernatural creative power. She has written a manual, called "Cultivating Kingdom Creativity," as well as her first book, *Born to Create*. For more information on these and other resources, and to view her ministry itinerary, visit her website: http://theresadedmonministries.com. She ministers with her husband, Kevin, and with their three children, Chad, Julia, and Alexa.

About Dawna DeSilva

Dawna DeSilva is the Founder and Leader of the International Healing and Deliverance Sozo Ministry birthed at Bethel Church. Dawna is also a leader of the Transformation Center at Bethel. Whether training pastors and leaders in Sozo, teaching on destiny, or ministering prophetically, she releases people, churches, and cities into new vision and freedom. No matter how traumatic the wounds in people's lives, Dawna ministers with authority and gentleness, imparting hope and healing.

Dawna travels nationally and internationally teaching Basic and Advanced Sozo seminars. She also teaches on the prophetic and physical healing. To find out more about Dawna's ministry and resources, visit the Sozo website: www.bethelsozo.com. Dawna and her husband, Steve, have three adult sons, and live in Redding, California.

About Jenn Johnson

Jenn Johnson and her husband, Brian, are the Senior Worship Pastors at Bethel Church, where they also oversee Bethel School of Worship, WorshipU, and Bethel Music. Their mission is for people to experience God's Kingdom and His manifest presence through worship. Brian and Jenn are featured on the Bethel Live Albums, as well as *The Loft Sessions,* and they have written many powerful songs, including "One Thing Remains," "Love Came Down," "God I look to You," and "O Taste and See." Their heart is to raise up strong leaders who are full of character and to teach people to view worship as not just music or singing, but to live "worship as a lifestyle." Jenn and Brian live in Redding, California, with their three wonderful children and spend their free time doing life with friends and family. For more information on Jenn's music and ministry, check out her website: www.jennjohnson.com; also visit www.BethelMusic.com to check out Jenn and Brian's worship music. Jenn would also love to interact with you via Twitter (@JennJohnson20) and Facebook (www.Facebook.com/BrianandJennJohnson).

ABOUT APRIL LAFRANCE

April is the Founder and CEO of OnDaySix (www.ondaysix. com), an online dating company that encourages social connection while delivering multimedia educational resources. The heart and vision is to empower Christians toward choosing one another with wisdom, through healthy dating, and teaching them how to love well.

As a fourth generation entrepreneur, April has a rich history in innovation and is responding to help turn the tide against one of the world's more pressing problems—the breakdown of families. She and the OnDaySix team have vision to influence and initiate the most powerful marriages that have ever walked the planet.

April is also a dynamic speaker whose practical wisdom and lively story-telling approach is helping to deliver the message of true hope for better relationships. She has been married for twelve years to the love of her life, Josh LaFrance. Together, in Northern California, they are loving and raising two incredible children—one biological son and one internationally adopted daughter. In her free time, April enjoys rock climbing, spending quality time with close friends, and traveling around the globe.

ABOUT BRITTNEY SERPELL

Brittney Serpell heads up the developing and training of the children and nursery staff at Bethel Church and oversees all Children's Department events. She is married to Ben Serpell, Bethel's Associate Youth Pastor, and they have two beautiful girls, Delani and Adalyn, and a son, Lincoln. Brittney has a passion to see people empowered by the relational and team-building tools that she teaches them. She is a master communicator, like her father, Danny Silk, author of *Loving Our Kids On Purpose,* and her mother, Sheri Silk, with whom she co-authored a chapter in this book. She has a wealth of knowledge beyond her age, having been raised in the Silk household. Brittney is also a certified parent educator through the Love and Logic Institute.

ABOUT JULIE WINTER

Julie Winter is a nurse practitioner with a Master's degree in nursing from UCLA. She currently works at a private family practice in Redding, California, and has over twenty-four years of experience in treating mood disorders. Julie also currently serves on the Bethel Church board, and it is her passion to help people find freedom from anxiety and depression. Julie and her husband, Mike, have two adult sons and one grandchild.

Recommended Reading

A Life of Miracles by Bill Johnson

Basic Training for the Prophetic Ministry by Kris Vallotton

Basic Training for the Supernatural Ways of Royalty by Kris Vallotton

Developing a Supernatural Lifestyle by Kris Vallotton

Dreaming With God by Bill Johnson

Face to Face by Bill Johnson

Here Comes Heaven by Bill Johnson and Mike Seth

Loving Our Kids On Purpose by Danny Silk

Moral Revolution by Kris Vallotton

Release the Power of Jesus by Bill Johnson

Strengthen Yourself in the Lord by Bill Johnson

The Happy Intercessor by Beni Johnson

Walking in the Supernatural by various Bethel authors

Born to Create by Theresa Dedmon

A Practical Guide to Evangelism – Supernaturally by Chris Overstreet

Kisses from a Good God by Paul Manwaring

The Supernatural Power of a Transformed Mind by Bill Johnson

The Supernatural Ways of Royalty by Kris Vallotton and Bill Johnson

Beautiful One by Beni Johnson and others

The Ultimate Treasure Hunt by Kevin Dedmon

Culture of Honor by Danny Silk

What on Earth is Glory by Paul Manwaring

The Risk Factor by Kevin Dedmon and Chad Dedmon

Practice of Honor by Danny Silk

Center of the Universe by Bill Johnson

Jesus Culture by Banning Liebscher

The Joy of Intercession by Beni Johnson

T.N.T. by Kevin Dedmon

An Apple for the Road by Bill Johnson, Paul Manwaring, Pam Spinosi and others

Unlocking Heaven by Kevin Dedmon

Journey of a World Changer by Banning Liebscher

Experiencing the Heavenly Realm by Beni Johnson and Judy Franklin

Hosting the Presence by Bill Johnson

I Am Your Sign by Sean Smith

Momentum by Bill Johnson and Eric Johnson

When Heaven Invades Earth by Bill Johnson

IN THE RIGHT HANDS, THIS BOOK WILL CHANGE LIVES!

Most of the people who need this message will not be looking for this book. To change their lives, you need to put a copy of this book in their hands.

> *But others (seeds) fell into good ground, and brought forth fruit, some a hundred-fold, some sixty-fold, some thirty-fold* (Matthew 13:8).

Our ministry is constantly seeking methods to find the good ground, the people who need this anointed message to change their lives. Will you help us reach these people?

> *Remember this—a farmer who plants only a few seeds will get a small crop. But the one who plants generously will get a generous crop* (2 Corinthians 9:6).

EXTEND THIS MINISTRY BY SOWING
3 BOOKS, 5 BOOKS, 10 BOOKS, **OR MORE TODAY,**
AND BECOME A LIFE CHANGER!

Thank you,

Don Nori Sr., Founder
Destiny Image
Since 1982